INSIGHT ⊙ GUIDES

EXPLORE

VANCOUVER & BC

PLAN & BOOK
YOUR TAILOR-MADE TRIP

BRAZIL

CHILE

ECUADOR

TAILOR-MADE TRIPS & UNIQUE EXPERIENCES CREATED BY LOCAL TRAVEL EXPERTS AT INSIGHTGUIDES.COM/HOLIDAYS

Insight Guides has been inspiring travellers with high-quality travel content for over 45 years. As well as our popular guidebooks, we now offer the opportunity to book tailor-made private trips completely personalised to your needs and interests.
By connecting with one of our local experts, you will directly benefit from their expertise and local know-how, helping you create memories that will last a lifetime.

HOW INSIGHTGUIDES.COM/HOLIDAYS WORKS

STEP 1

Pick your dream destination and submit an enquiry, or modify an existing itinerary if you prefer.

STEP 2

Fill in a short form, sharing details of your travel plans and preferences with a local expert.

STEP 3

Your local expert will create your personalised itinerary, which you can amend until you are completely satisfied.

STEP 4

Book securely online. Pack your bags and enjoy your holiday! Your local expert will be available to answer questions during your trip.

HISTORY BUFFS

Explore where present-day Vancouver began in Gastown (route 2) and delve into Indigenous history and culture at the Museum of Anthropology (route 5) and visit the seat of the provincial government in Victoria (route 10).

SHOPPING

Robson Street in Vancouver has a wide range of stores (route 1), or explore the artisan studios of Railspur Alley on Granville Island (route 3). The trip to the Cowichan Valley and Nanaimo includes small towns noted for their art and craft galleries (route 12).

SPORTY TYPES

Whistler (route 7) has all the facilities for both summer and winter sports. In Vancouver, you can rent a bike and cycle the Seawall (route 1). Tofino (route 13) is the place for surfing and sea kayaking.

VIEWS

High points in Vancouver and Victoria include the Vancouver Lookout (route 1), the Eye of the Wind at Grouse Mountain (route 6), and Gonzales Hill (route 11). Stunning driving roads include the Sea-to-Sky Highway (route 7) and Hwy-1 from Revelstoke to the Rockies (route 9).

INTRODUCTION

An introduction to Vancouver and BC's geography, customs and culture, plus illuminating background information on cuisine, history and what to do when you're there.

Aerial view of downtown Vancouver

EXPLORE VANCOUVER AND BC

British Columbia is a land of snow-capped summits, rivers and forests
Its two biggest urban areas are Vancouver, known for its laidback
lifestyle, and Victoria, a devotedly anglophile provincial capital.

Vancouver is the largest city in Western Canada, lively in an easy-going way, and sophisticated but not above making fun of itself. A multicultural beacon of tolerance and inclusivity, it is consistently ranked as one of the best cities in the world. The population is noted for its healthy and active lifestyle and for high levels of environmental awareness – Greenpeace was founded here in 1971. It's not just aware either, it puts its money where its mouth is: 95 percent of its electricity is supplied by renewable energy. It is also the third-largest movie and TV production center in North America, earning it the nickname it shares with Toronto: 'Hollywood North'.

Off its west coast is Vancouver Island, a microcosm of the province's immense natural riches and home to Victoria, the provincial capital of British Columbia, which was established in colonial times and retains a modicum of 'Englishness', with its refined afternoon teas and British-style pubs. Like Vancouver, it scores highly on environmental awareness issues and is home to a health-conscious and active population – the city is often referred to as the 'cycling capital of Canada' for having the highest proportion of bicycle-riding residents per capita.

It's well worth journeying over to the island's west and north coasts and sailing to Prince Rupert. BC's interior has Canada's only semi-arid desert, an award-winning wine region, superb backcountry skiing, and epic – though decreasing – glaciers, and northern BC is stark and remote, but with the luxury of a backcountry that you can explore by road, and sea journeys that rate among the most breath-taking in Canada.

GEOGRAPHY AND LAYOUT

Vancouver

With Burrard Inlet to the north, English Bay to the west, Vancouver Harbour to the east, and False Creek cutting to the southern section, the downtown core of Vancouver can almost seem like an island. But the metropolitan area stretches far beyond, encompassing 21 municipalities and covering 2,930 sq km (1,131 sq miles).

The road pattern is in a grid, except where large parks get in the way, with streets (which are named) running north–south and avenues (which are

The popular Gassy Jack statue, Gastown

numbered, except for Broadway and King Edward Avenue) running east–west. Avenues also have 'East' or 'West' attached, depending on which side of Ontario Street they are on.

Vancouver's downtown core is quite compact and very walkable, but there is an excellent transit system that includes buses, the SkyTrain system, the SeaBus, and the False Creek ferries.

Victoria

Victoria is smaller and even more walkable. Centered on its lovely inner harbour on the southwestern extremity of Vancouver Island, it faces south toward the Strait of Juan de Fuca and the US state of Washington. It also has a comprehensive bus service within and beyond the downtown area.

Both cities offer sightseeing buses, cruises, floatplane flights, and whale-watching trips. Taxis are also plentiful.

HISTORY

For more than 10,000 years the Coast Salish people have called this area home, with the Salishan and Nuu-chah-nulth (formerly referred to as Nootka) groups predominating around the province's southwest coast and Vancouver Island. Northwest culture was generally peaceful and diplomatic, with disputes often solved with gifts rather than aggression. Art was, and still is, very important within the culture, and superb examples of Coast Salish's distinctive style of painting, carving, masks, woven goods, and basketry can be found in museums, galleries, and craft shops throughout the region.

The arrival of Europeans began with the Spanish, followed later by Captain James Cook searching for the Northwest Passage in the 1770s, with a young George Vancouver in his crew. George was to return in 1792, this time captaining his own vessel and charting the coastline of the island and the part of the mainland that would take his name. The sailors took home stories of the vast forests and the furs they had seen, prompting the arrival of loggers and trappers on a quest for these lucrative materials.

The furs were traded by the North-West Trading Company and its rival, the Hudson's Bay Company; the latter still

Covid-19 updates

In early 2020, Covid-19 swept across the globe, being categorized as a pandemic by the World Health Organization in March 2020. While travelling in Canada, be sure to heed all local laws, travel advice and hygiene measures; flouting these means risking your own health but can also put a strain on local communities and their medical infrastructure. While we've done all we can to make sure this guide is accurate and up to date, permanent closures and changed opening hours are likely in the wake of coronavirus, so be sure to check ahead.

Orcas spotted on a whale-watching tour

has a chain of department stores across Canada, popularly known as 'The Bay'. The forests provided much-needed lumber, much of which was transported back to Europe. Western red cedar was in demand because of its natural resistance to rot, and pin-straight Douglas fir trunks were used for the masts of sailing ships. The first sawmill in this part of the world was established where Victoria now stands, and the second was on the site now occupied by Vancouver. It was very demanding work, and all those loggers and fur trappers got extremely thirsty; enter Gassy Jack Deighton (see page 35), who opened a saloon and later a hotel to cater to this demand. A small town began to grow up around it, which came to be known as Gassy's Town – today's Gastown area of Vancouver.

Gold was discovered in various parts of British Columbia in the mid 1800s, bringing in hordes of prospectors along with people who could make a living providing services to them. These rich pickings encouraged Britain to create a colony and develop what would become the province of British Columbia. Periods of boom and bust followed, but recent history has shown the economy to be consistently on an upward trend. This has boosted and been boosted by immigration, particularly from China, which has helped to create a model of well-integrated multiculturalism that is the envy of cities worldwide.

CLIMATE

The southwestern parts of **British Columbia** enjoy some of Canada's best weather: the extremes are less marked and the overall temperatures generally milder than elsewhere. Much of the province, though, bears the brunt of Pacific depressions, so this is one of the country's damper regions: it can be very wet in the cities from November through March – many hotels routinely provide umbrellas for all their guests – but this means temperatures remain above freezing, around the mid- to upper 40s°F (6–10°C). And, as the rest of Canada says, at least you don't have to shovel it.

Head out of town and up into higher altitudes, though, and it's a different story – the ski resorts depend on good amounts of the right kind of snow, after all, and some of North America's finest slopes and amenities are just 100km (64 miles)

Indigenous BC

This travel guide describes places that include the traditional lands and unceded territories of many Indigenous Peoples, including 198 distinct First Nations who have lived here for over 10,000 years. Travelling offers us the privilege of being a guest among our hosts and building relationships with them. As you travel, take the opportunity to learn the history of a place; support Indigenous businesses and artists; and make connections with the people who continue to inhabit these lands.

A great turnout at Sunset Beach Park to listen to the Vancouver Symphony Orchestra

or so away from Vancouver at the Whistler-Blackcomb resort, which co-hosted the 2010 Winter Olympic Games.

Spring and fall are lovely, with temperatures around the upper 50s and low 60s°F (14–17°C), and summer usually sees temperature around the low 70s°F (21–23°C), although it can climb above 80°F (26°C) and heatwaves can bring the danger of wildfires in forested areas.

POPULATION

Almost half of the 5.1 million people who live in British Columbia were born elsewhere, but the province remains one of the least densely populated in the country. British Columbia has long been home to Indigenous peoples including First Nations, Inuit, and Métis. There are 198 distinct First Nations in BC, each with their own unique traditions and history.

Vancouver
At the latest count in 2021, 2.6 million people call the Greater Vancouver area home, with 631,500 living in the city itself. The cultural diversity is remarkable, with more than half of the popula-

DON'T LEAVE VANCOUVER AND BRITISH COLUMBIA WITHOUT...

Taking a harbour boat tour. For stunning views over the water and back to the cityscape. Both Vancouver and Victoria have numerous options for getting out onto the water, from cruises with meals to zippy Zodiac tours in search of whales. See pages 42 and 86.

Walking or cycling along the Seawall. For more splendid views and the company of like-minded locals and visitors. The easy, level route hugs the shoreline, links numerous attractions and parks, and there are bike rentals plus the Mobi bike-share service in useful locations. See pages 31 and 43.

Admiring superlative Indigenous art. At the Museum of Anthropology or Bill Reid Art Gallery in Vancouver, the Royal BC Museum in Victoria. See pages 47, 31, and 74.

Taking a traditional English-style after-noon tea at Victoria's stately Fairmont Empress Hotel. A long-held tradition in elegant historic surroundings that are reputed to be haunted. See page 107.

Sampling a craft beer or award-winning wine. Try Yaletown Brewing Company in Vancouver and Cedar Creek Estate Winery near Kelowna. See page 63.

Spotting a grizzly bear. BC is home to half of Canada's grizzly bears: head to Khutzeymateen Grizzly Sanctuary from Prince Rupert. See page 97.

Gazing at a Glacier. Illecillewaet can be viewed from the highway, or up close from hiking trails in Glacier National Park. See page 67.

Eating at a Food Truck. Tacos, smoothies, grilled cheese sandwiches, and Japanese style hot dogs top the list of delicious dishes to taste. See page 110.

Victoria's Legislative Assembly building, beautifully lit up in the evening

tion having a mother tongue other than English. It has the largest population of Chinese people of any city in North America, and one of the largest Chinatowns in the world. There are also significant numbers of people originating from the Indian subcontinent, the Philippines, and Korea as well as some from the US, the UK, and the Netherlands.

Victoria

Victoria has a population of 378,170, mostly of British descent, but with Chinese, South Asian, German, and Punjabi people too.

LOCAL CUSTOMS

The people of Vancouver and British Columbia are extremely polite, friendly, and helpful. Locals are really congenial and there's no doubt that you'll strike up many conversations with them – take an interest in hockey (ice-hockey) and develop a passion for coffee and you'll fit right in.

In 2018, Translink, the public transit operator, announced an etiquette campaign. In addition to the obvious, they issue advice at www.translink.ca/Rider-Guide/Etiquette-on-Transit.aspx that is well worth checking out. On escalators, you should stand on the right to allow people in a hurry to pass on the left. In a city that suffers so much rain, umbrella etiquette is highly valued – be mindful of those around you when opening one up or shaking one off.

POLITICS AND ECONOMICS

There are a lot of registered political parties in British Columbia – 15 at the last count – ranging from national parties like the Conservative Party, Liberal Party, Green Party, and New Democratic Party, to those that could come under the 'lunatic fringe' category with outfits like the Work Less Party and the Marijuana Party. At the provincial level, the New Democratic Party, with a social democratic platform, is currently in power, headed by Premier John Horgan, and Janet Austin is the Lieutenant Governer. Vancouver's current mayor, Kennedy Stewart, is an independent. Victoria's city mayor is Lisa Helps (a great name for a politician), also an independent, who was re-elected in 2018. Party support depends to some extent on levels of affluence, with higher-income residents leaning towards the center-right and less well-off people supporting the left, but there's an emerging trend toward the left across the board.

The economy, aided by an active Economic Commission, is thriving, based on a diverse range of sectors from technology to tourism to business services to the movie industry, and much else besides. Entrepreneurship here is alive and well.

The way of life in Vancouver and BC has created a generally happy, contented, and outgoing population, and that quickly rubs off on visitors. Without even speaking to anyone, there seems to be a tangible feel of contentment in the air –

Surfers on Long Beach, Pacific Rim National Park Reserve

unless, that is, you've wandered into one of the very few wrong parts of town in the big cities; as everywhere, these do exist, but are very localized and easily avoided. Whether it's the climate, the stunning surroundings, the range of attractions and activities, the healthy lifestyle, or a combination of them all, these cities never fail to delight. But if, as often happens, you fall in love with these places and have a mind to relocate, you will soon discover a downside – the cost of real estate. Vancouver was cited in September 2018 by the Swiss investment bank UBS as having one of the world's biggest housing bubbles, and it's not letting up. Prices are high in Victoria too, which is another indication of their huge popularity.

TOP TIPS FOR VISITING VANCOUVER AND BRITISH COLUMBIA

Forward planning. The amount of choice for things to do here can seem overwhelming, so spend a bit of time in advance of your trip working out your own preferences and priorities. Try to factor in a bit of down time, though, to just hang out where the locals gather and get a real feel for the character of the place.

To rent or not to rent a car? Public transit is excellent in Vancouver and Victoria and there are various handy travel passes. While it's possible to use public transport to get around the province, it's likely that you'll want a car.

Fireworks. If you're in Vancouver during the International Celebration of Light fireworks competition, Vanier Park and English Bay offer the best viewing. Go early to secure a good spot.

Provincial holidays. British Columbia has five provincial holidays, when most businesses and organisations are closed: Family Day (third Monday in February), Victoria Day (Monday before May 25), British Columbia Day (first Monday in August), Thanksgiving (second Monday in October), and Remembrance Day (November 11). Easter Sunday, Easter Monday and Boxing Day are not statutory holidays in BC.

Cruise crowds. When planning to visit a popular attraction, it's worth checking the cruise ship schedule. Vancouver welcomes close to a million cruise passengers a year in its May through September season, but even in the highest season there are some days with no ships in port, meaning the top places to visit will be less crowded.

Half-price tickets. Theatres, comedy clubs, and sporting venues often offer half-price admission via Tourism Vancouver's Tickets Tonight website (www.ticketstonight. ca), available on the day of performance between 9am and 4pm, with a maximum of four tickets per person.

'Green' tourism. If you worry about the carbon footprint of your sightseeing trips, you might want to try the zero-emissions boat tours and generally more sustainable tours that are available in BC. Some floatplane sightseeing and whale-watching operators offset their carbon emissions and Harbour Air is developing electric airplanes. Ask your hotel about their carbon footprint.

Afternoon tea at the Fairmont Empress

FOOD AND DRINK

When it comes to eating well, the locals definitely have your back here. Because of their passion for fresh, healthy ingredients and their eclectic culinary tastes, you'll find a huge variety of top-quality local and international cuisines in many types of eateries.

British Columbia residents are, in general, extremely discerning – whether it's a fine-dining restaurant, a food truck, pub-grub, or a doughnut shop, they will have an opinion about which is best. This has resulted in a lot of lively discussion, but, more importantly, it means that the province has many high-quality places to eat and drink covering every price range.

The locavore movement continues to thrive here too, and you just need to visit one of the public markets or farmers' markets to witness the huge support for fresh, local, organic, sustainably grown, and ethically farmed or fished ingredients. And the shoppers are not just local residents stocking their larders – chefs from nearby restaurants visit on a daily basis to get first pick of what's freshest and best, and their menus may proudly include details of where ingredients have been sourced.

When it comes to drinking, you'll have a choice of locally brewed beers, locally distilled spirits, and wines from British Columbia's vineyards alongside plenty of the world's finest imported beverages. And then there's the coffee…

GOURMET COFFEE SCENE

The people of Vancouver, in particular, were passionate about coffee long before it became a trend. Discerning European immigrants brought their coffee traditions with them and from this has grown a serious coffee culture that has become a real passion. Look beyond the ubiquitous Tim Horton's and Starbucks and seek out the serious coffee houses and champion baristas – indeed, making coffee is a competitive art, and one of Vancouver's best-known baristas, Sammy Piccolo, is a four-time Canadian Barista Champion. His Prado Café in East Vancouver would make an excellent place to start your search for the best brew. Commercial Drive has several coffee spots, although it's away from the downtown area. Names to look out for around the city include Milano Coffee, a few blocks southwest of Olympic Village, Forty Ninth Parallel Café and Lucky's Doughnuts on Thurlow Street, and Gastown's Revolver Coffee.

Victoria is known for its English-style afternoon teas, most notably at The Empress Hotel, but it has

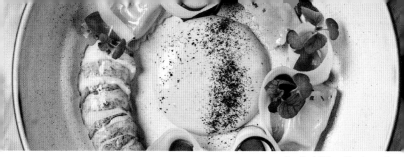

A seafood dish at Hawksworth

a good coffee scene too, with some great independent coffee shops like Discovery Coffee, which has a couple of downtown locations, two more and their roastery farther out, and a truck. The area around Fan Tan Alley has some that are worth seeking out too – try Habit Coffee. Coffee culture has spread to all the urban areas of BC and you're never far away from a roastery and a superb batch brew.

WHERE TO EAT

Restaurant types in BC are incredibly wide-ranging in scope, with Indigenous, West Coast and seafood cuisines on offer alongside (in the big cities, at least) European, Indian, Middle and Far Eastern, North and South American, and African. Vegetarian, vegan, and gluten-free diets are all covered in urban areas too (though less so in remote areas), and chefs range from celebrity icons to talented self-taught cooks serving up comfort food from traditional recipes.

The term 'spoilt for choice' could have been invented specifically for Vancouver. **Yaletown** is one of the gastronomic hotspots, with several of the city's finest-dining options as well as gastro-pubs and great cafés. **Gastown** is known for its good range of eateries, and **Chinatown** of course has places serving authentic cuisine. **Granville Island** not only has the Market Grill in its wonderful Public Market,

but also several nearby eateries that source their ingredients there. **Downtown**, especially where the most chic boutiques are located, offers fine dining as well, with an enormous variety of places for shoppers to refuel along Robson Street and its hinterland. On the west side of Vancouver, Kitsilano is another spot with a reputation for good restaurants, as well as the Organic Villa Food Truck that can sometimes be found parked near the beach.

As the provincial capital, it goes without saying that **Victoria** has high-end choices to cater to the discerning needs of politicians and visiting dignitaries. What doesn't go without saying is that the general public can eat in the restaurant at the **Legislative Assembly** building, albeit with a security check and some restrictions on when you can go (see page 73). Another highlight in BC's capital is the afternoon tea served at the **Fairmont Empress Hotel** fronting the harbour. It's a real throwback to colonial times, with elegant surroundings, 21 varieties of tea to choose from, and all the traditional British fare that's fit for (and has been served to) royalty. Elsewhere on Vancouver Island, tiny **Nanaimo** and **Tofino** have food scenes that punch well above their weight. Heading to the east of the province, the **Okanagan** has become a destination for travellers from far and wide for its wineries and outstanding vineyard restaurants, and ski-season in **Whistler** brings

You're never far away from a Tim Hortons

big spenders to its high-end restaurants. Almost everywhere in BC you'll find food trucks (see page 110), and although many of the trucks are well established, others may come and go in every sense of the phrase.

High-end restaurants

BC cities (and especially Vancouver) are home to a number of world-class restaurants, often with celebrity chefs at the helm, that offer a dining experience to remember. Sophisticated dining rooms and immaculately set tables set the scene for artistically presented dishes and the finest wines, though stuffy restaurants are very rarely seen on the west coast. These settings are more than backed up by the food on the plates, with flavourful creations based on the finest local seafood, meats and fresh produce you could imagine.

Spots to look out for in Vancouver are the Blue Water Café, Tojo's, and Hawksworth. In Victoria, head for Q at the Empress, The Dining Room, and the Harbour House Restaurant.

Food and drink prices

Price for a two-course meal for one including a glass of wine (or other beverage)
$ = under $20
$$ = $20–45
$$$ = $45–60
$$$$ = over $60

International restaurants

The multicultural make-up of Vancouver and Victoria has resulted in a wonderful array of really authentic cuisines from across the globe. Both cities have Chinatowns where you'll find excellent dim sum, also known as 'yum cha' (because it's served with plenty of tea) and other Oriental specialties. Vancouver's Floata Seafood Restaurant is Canada's largest Chinese restaurant. There's spectacular sushi also – Vancouver was one of the first Western cities to introduce this Japanese specialty, and it's now a favourite across the province. Tojo's has been one of its foremost exponents for some 50 years. On Vancouver Island, try Azuma Sushi or the Senzushi Japanese Restaurant & Sushi Bar in Victoria, Nori Japanes Restaurant in Nanaimo, and Wasabiya Japanese Sushi Café in Campbell River.

Indian food is big too, brought by South Asian communities and still most often found in family-run restaurants. These are good places to find interesting vegetarian dishes.

In addition, you'll find Italian, French, Mexican, South American, Caribbean, Greek, and Mediterranean restaurants – and various fusions of these.

Pubs

There's quite a lot a variety in the style of the pubs in BC, and although few get close to the norm on the other side of the Atlantic, there's good food

Canada's favorite, poutine

A colourful selection at Craig Street Brew Pub

in many of them. You'll also find some exceptionally fine beers, especially in the brewpubs that make their own on the premises. BC has more than 125 breweries and counting, and even pubs that don't brew their own will often carry craft beers from local sources, local wines, and even locally distilled spirits.

Lots of pubs that aren't actually foodie destinations will serve perfectly enjoyable fare, usually of the fairly standard fish-and-chips, chicken, and burgers variety.

INDIGENOUS CUISINE

Knowledge and interest in Indigenous culinary traditions are being revived in BC and places are springing up where you can sample menus inspired by traditional Indigenous, pre-colonial ingredients and cooking methods.

In Vancouver, track down the Mr Bannock Food Truck in North Van or reserve a table at Salmon n' Bannock Bistro on West Broadway (bannock bread is an Indigenous staple traditionally made from corn or flour, a must-eat while you're in BC). Also make a beeline for Kekuli Café in the Okanagan's Merritt, which is owned and operated by Elijah Mack from the Nixalk Nation of Bella Coola.

FOODIE TOURS

Food tours are a great way to discover the best eating experiences, with several companies approaching this from different angles. Tour operators include Vancouver Food Tour (www.vancouverfoodtour.com) offering eight options, Vancouver Foodie Tours (www.foodietours.ca) and Taste Vancouver (www.tastevancouverfoodtours.com), each with four tours, and Off the Eaten Track (www.offtheeatentracktours.ca), with three tours. In Victoria, get in touch with Spirit Culinary Excursions (www.spiritculinaryexcursions.com) for food tours of Vancouver Island. Elsewhere, the land of "beaches, peaches, sunshine and wine" (the Okanagan), is ripe for food and winery tours – contact Okanagan Foodie Tours (www.okanaganfoodietours.ca).

Dine Out Vancouver

Over the space of 17 days from mid-January to early February, this festival promotes a huge range of food-related events, including guided tours, demonstrations, talks, cooking classes, tastings, and street food. More than 250 restaurants take part by offering fixed-price menus with pairings based on British Columbia wines, craft beers, and other drinks, and some organize a chef-exchange with restaurants in Europe. Many Vancouver hotels offer special festival rates too. For more information visit www.dineoutvancouver.com.

Celebrating with a bang: the Celebration of Light fireworks in Vancouver

ENTERTAINMENT

Whether you want to soak up some culture, laugh it up at a comedy club, or listen to a band in an arena or a pub, you'll find what you're looking for in British Columbia.

Vancouver is the entertainment hotspot for the province, but Victoria too has plenty going on when the sun goes down. Elsewhere in BC, smaller cities have their own theatres, and plenty of rural and urban communities host local cultural events year-round.

Celebration of Light

One of the biggest summer events in Vancouver, held over eight days in late July and early August, this is a huge fireworks event in which three countries complete to elicit the loudest 'oohs' and 'aahs' from the crowd. The most spectacular fireworks displays you may ever have seen, set off from a barge floating in the bay, are accompanied by synchronized music, with the explosions high above providing the loudest percussion. If you are lucky or important enough, you can reserve a spot in the VIP area, but most folks bring a picnic and grab a piece of ground around English Bay and the Burrard Inlet. While they are waiting for the main event, there are bands on stage all afternoon. Full details are available on https://hondacelebrationoflight.com or from the tourist office.

VANCOUVER

Vancouver claims a world-class symphony orchestra, as well as opera, theatre, and dance companies at the cutting edge of contemporary arts. It's on every major tour itinerary, from the biggest names in rock and country music to opera icons. Festivals proliferate throughout summer while numerous music venues provide a hotbed of up-and-coming rock bands and a well-established jazz scene. Comprehensive listings appear in the Georgia Straight (www.straight.com), a free weekly newspaper available across the city. Half-price and last-minute tickets are available via "Tickets Tonight" (www.ticketstonight.ca) at the main visitor center at 200 Burrard Street.

Theatre

The city actively promotes the arts, and owns several theatres: the Queen Elizabeth, hosting Broadway-style musicals and the like; the Orpheum, a grand and elegant concert hall, home to the Vancouver Symphony and hosting international visiting artists; the Vancouver Playhouse, a more intimate theater for recitals and dance groups; and the cab-

A performance at the Chan Centre for the Performing Arts

aret-style Annex for contemporary and avant-garde dance and musical performances. The University of British Columbia campus has several venues too, notably the splendid Chan Centre. Other theaters include the Firehall Arts Centre on East Cordova Street and the Roundhouse in Yaletown.

Among the many theatre companies, the Arts Club performs at the Stanley Theatre on Granville Street and at the Granville Island Stage, next door to the Public Market, and Touchstone Theatre produces around three shows a year.

Comedy and live venues

There are several comedy venues, including a branch of the Yuk Yuks chain on Cambie Street and The Comedy Mix on Burrard, and the Vancouver TheatreSports League, which performs live improv every night on Granville Island.

Numerous smaller-scale venues for live music of many kinds can be found all over the city. They include arts centers, pubs, clubs, breweries, cafés, restaurants, churches (St James' has a music series) and hotel lobbies and bars – https://livevan.com is a good source for what's on. With the largest LGBTQ+ community in Western Canada, there's no shortage of friendly venues to choose from, and Commercial Drive and Davie Village are good places to begin, the latter including the renowned Numbers Cabaret.

The city takes it outside in the summer, to park amphitheaters like the Malkin Bowl and the Theatre under the Stars in Stanley Park and Vanier Park respectively, the area outside the CBC building on Hamilton Street, and on the plaza outside the Queen Elizabeth Theatre.

VICTORIA

Theatre

The city is home to Victoria's Symphony, the Canadian Pacific Ballet, Pacific Opera Victoria, the Victoria Civic Orchestra, and several theaters: the Royal Theatre, McPherson Playhouse, Langham Court Theatre, Kaleidoscope Theatre, Belfry Theatre, and the little Metro Studio Theatre. The University of Victoria puts on concerts and plays in the Farquhar Auditorium, the Young Recital Hall, and the Phoenix Theatres.

Music, dance, comedy

There's buzzing nightlife too, including the long-established Hermann's Jazz Club and the Capital Ballroom, which has a full calendar of touring acts and local shows. For those who like to dance, there are a couple of high-tech DJ dance clubs, including Paparazzi, which caters to the 'alternative' and LGBTQ+ crowd. For those who prefer to listen, there's a long list of live music pubs and clubs catering to many genres, including Lucky Bar on Yates Street. There's comedy at Hecklers Bar and Grill on Gorge Road E. It's worth checking out the churches and cathedrals too, notably Christ Church Cathedral and the First Metropolitan United Church, where shows are often by donation.

Kayakers enjoying a beautiful sunrise near Kitsilano Beach

ACTIVITIES AND SPORTS

Most Canadians love nothing more than the outdoor life and British Columbia has a plethora of active pursuits to offer, whether you want to hop on a bike, zipline from a mountain top, or just watch a hockey game.

SPECTATOR SPORTS

The atmosphere that fills the big arenas during home games is quite an experience. If you're in Vancouver between mid-September and April, it's worth getting tickets for a Vancouver Canucks NHL (National Hockey League) game at the Rogers Arena (http://tickets.canucks.com) – enquire early as they sell out fast The junior WHL (Western Hockey League) is a decent alternative and fun to watch; check out the Kamloops Blazers (www.blazerhockey.com), Kelowna Rockets (www.kelownarockets.com), Vancouver Giants (www.vancouvergiants.com) and Victoria Royals (www.victoriaroyals.com).

Summer spectator sports include football (www.bclions.com), soccer (www.whitecapsfc.com), baseball (www.milb.com/vancouver), and lacrosse (www.vancouverlacrosse.com).

There are dozens of yacht clubs in BC, and their races are a fine sight, particularly those between the Royal Yacht Clubs in Vancouver (www.royalvan.com) and Victoria (www.rvyc.org.uk). Also see the Victoria City Rowing Club (www.vcrc.bc.ca), which hosts the BC Championships + Challenge West event in July.

For a more casual spectator event, why not catch a dragon boat race? The major event is the Concord Pacific Dragon Boat Festival in June when around 5,500 paddlers propel their boats around False Creek in Vancouver.

WATER SPORTS

There are plenty of options for getting on or into the water here – from setting out on a water bike or in a kayak, to taking a whale-watching or fishing trip. For kayaking or paddleboarding in Vancouver, Jericho Beach Kayak Centre (www.jerichobeachkayak.com) provides rentals, tuition, and tours, and Vancouver Water Adventures (www.vancouverwateradventures.com) offers a similar service on Granville Island and Kitsilano Beach.

ADRENALIN RUSH

Experiences to take your breath away include bungee jumping over spectacular rapids at Whistler (https://whistlerbungee.com) and paragliding and ziplining at the top of Grouse Mountain (www.grousemountain.com). There are treetop adventures at Kitsilano (www.cap

Skiing in Whistler

bridge.com) and Nanaimo, which have you clambering up log ladders, crossing wobbly plank bridges, and swinging through the trees on ropes. On Vancouver Island there's ziplining at Sooke, about 40km (25 miles) west of Victoria, operated by Adrenaline (https://adrenalinezip.com). Skydiving is also popular and available in the Okanagan (www.okanaganskydive.com) and Nanoose Bay (www.skydivevancouverisland.com), as well as Vancouver and Whistler.

WALKING AND HIKING

From a pleasant stroll around the Vancouver Seawall to strenuous backcountry hiking on Vancouver Island, there are countless opportunities to use your feet. Most rewarding, if you have the stamina, is to get out into the wilderness and trek through stunning scenery to breathtaking viewpoints; a good option close to the city is the Pacific Spirit Regional Park. The strenuous West Coast Trail on Vancouver Island is on many people's bucket lists. There are many guided hiking trips available too, including Step Outside Adventures (www.soadventures.com) and Coastal Bliss Hiking Tours (www.coastalbliss.ca), but if you prefer to strike out and explore independently, various hikes are detailed on www.outdoorvancouver.ca. See www.backcountrylodgesofbc.com to find a lodge and obtain the appropriate 1:50,000 sheet from the Canadian Topographical Series.

GOLF

There are many golf courses in British Columbia (www.britishcolumbiagolf.org). There are four courses in Vancouver itself, and several more in the surrounding districts – Capilano is regarded as one of the best in the province. Victoria has even more within or in easy reach of the city (https://golfvancouverisland.ca). As in many places, the finest courses are private, but many excellent ones are welcoming to visitors.

WINTER SPORTS

Although Vancouver and Vancouver Island don't get as cold as other places, on the higher elevations in Whistler and the BC Rockies there will be snow aplenty. Whistler, has world-class facilities; full details can be found on www.whistler.com/activities/winter. Other excellent ski resorts include Kicking Horse Mountain Resort (kickinghorseresort.com), just west of Golden, and Big White Ski Resort (www.bigwhite.com), 56 km (35 miles) southeast of Kelowna.

Options within easy reach of Vancouver include Cypress Mountain (www.cypressmountain.com), Mount Seymour (https://mtseymour.ca), and Grouse Mountain (www.grousemountain.com), all of which have downhill runs, ski lifts, rentals and tuition. And there's always the annual New Year's Day Polar Bear Swim in English Bay – a frigid 100-metre race with participants in fancy dress.

BEST ROUTES

WATERFRONT AND DOWNTOWN

Begin on Vancouver's stunning waterfront, with its top-class attractions and superlative views. Follow this with a stroll in the heart of Downtown to see incredible works of art, before relaxing in Vancouver Library's pretty rooftop garden.

DISTANCE: 4.1km (2.5 miles)
TIME: 4–5 hours
START: Vancouver Lookout
END: Vancouver Central Library
POINTS TO NOTE: Fly Over Canada gives discounts for online ticket purchase, but you will still have to line up to get in, and lines extend out of the building, so be prepared for the weather. The Vancouver Lookout may also offer savings for online ticket purchase (tickets are valid all day). The Bill Reid Gallery is closed on Monday and Tuesday. The cathedral is a weekday option, unless you're attending a service, and it's worth checking the website for details of any concerts and/or rehearsals of their choir. Photographers take note: tripods are not allowed on the Lookout's deck.

If you arrive by car, there's parking beside Waterfront Station and in the Parkade on West Cordova Street, beneath the Harbour Centre. If using public transportation, make for Waterfront Station, which serves the SkyTrain, the West Coast Express and the Seabus.

There's always plent of activity on the Waterfront, and when the sun goes down you can go back up the Lookout to watch the city lights come on, then head back to Canada Place to see the Sails of Light illuminated. Downtown is best visited during the day when you can do some window shopping on Robson Street, visit BC's best galleries and take in Christchurch Cathedral.

VANCOUVER LOOKOUT

On the block opposite Waterfront Station, the **Vancouver Lookout** ❶ (http://vancouverlookout.com; May–Oct daily 8.30am–10.30pm; Oct–May daily 9am–9pm, except for special closures) offers a fine 360-degree view over the city and to the mountains beyond. It is well worth the price – particularly as you can return as many times as you like within the day. Ideally, you'd start the day here to orient

Sunset seen from the Vancouver Lookout

yourself, then return to watch the sun go down.

A glass elevator whisks you up to the Observation Deck, nearly 169 meters (553ft) above the city. Outward-sloping windows give you a clear view directly downward, and there are telescopes to bring the landmarks into closer view. You can also enjoy the view while having a meal at the Top of Vancouver.

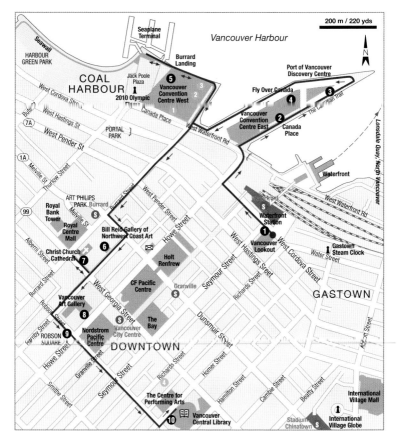

Canada Place

CANADA PLACE

Back down on West Cordova Street, walk left passing Waterfront Station on your right, then at Howe Street turn right to reach **Canada Place ❷**. On the exact spot where some of the earliest explorers came ashore, this futuristic development opened in 1986 as the Canada Pavilion for the Expo 86 World Fair, and is now an architectural icon.

When you are finally able to take your eyes off the water and the mountains that lie on the other side, walk the perimeter of Canada Place to explore the **Canadian Trail ❸**. A series of interactive exhibits provide information about each of Canada's 10 provinces and three territories.

Sightseeing Flights

If the Lookout isn't high enough for you, you can take one of the seaplane pleasure flights offered by Harbour Air Seaplanes (tel: 1-800-665 0212; www. harbourair.com), from a quick 10-minute flight over the harbour, Downtown, and Stanley Park to full-day and multi-day tours. Choices include flying over to Victoria then taking a whale-watching boat ride, flying over mountains and glaciers then landing on a remote alpine lake, and a trip to Horseshoe Bay for a boat tour and a meal. The price includes a carbon offset fee and Harbour Air plan to go all-electric within a few years.

You will probably have spotted seaplanes taking off and landing nearby. To get a taste of the experience without leaving the ground, head for **Fly Over Canada ❹** (www.flyovercanada. com; daily 10am–9pm, every 15–20 minutes). Once you are safely secured into your seat, the floor drops away so that your legs dangle freely. As the projection onto the surrounding 20-metre (66ft) spherical screen begins, the whole structure moves; you'll feel as if you are flying over some of Canada's most iconic scenery. The ride takes about eight minutes.

BURRARD LANDING AND JACK POOLE PLAZA

From Canada Place, walk past the Vancouver Convention Centre West to reach **Burrard Landing ❺** and Jack Poole Plaza. The Convention Centre hosts hundreds of events every year, including Art Vancouver every April, the Vancouver International Wine Festival in March, and a huge Christmas Market. Vancouver's famous Seawall (see page 31) begins here too; walking its length is a popular pastime for residents and visitors alike.

On Jack Poole Plaza, the Olympic Cauldron structure is an impressive work of art, as is the remarkable Digital Orca sculpture by local artist Douglas Coupland. If you're around after dark, you'll see the myriad tiny lights embedded in it, blinking in sequence.

Cycling along the Seawall in Stanley Park

If hunger pangs are setting in, try the **Coal Harbour Café**, see ❶, or for something more substantial, visit the **Bellaggio Café**, see ❷. If you prefer to picnic, take-out food is available from **Mahony & Sons**, see ❸. Green spaces include Harbour Green Park or the locals' choice, Art Philips Park, a delightful oasis that's glorious when the cherry trees are in bloom.

BILL REID GALLERY OF NORTHWEST COASTAL ART

Walk 0.5km south on Burrard Street, turn left on Dunsmuir Street and immediately right on Hornby Street; the gallery is on the block between Dunsmuir and W Georgia streets. The **Bill Reid Gallery of Northwest Coastal Art** ❻ (tel: 604-682-3455; www.billreidgallery. ca; Wed–Sun 11am–5pm) is dedicated to contemporary Indigenous Northwest Coast art. The small collection contains magnificent works set out in a light-filled space. The works of Bill Reid form the core of the collection, and regular temporary exhibitions explore other artists and media, such as cultural tattoos or Indigenous crafts. There are also arts and crafts workshops, artist talks, and events for children.

CHRIST CHURCH CATHEDRAL

From the Bill Reid Gallery, walk along Hornby to West Georgia Street and turn right; continue to the corner of Burrard Street.

On the northeast corner of West Georgia and Burrard, the Gothic-Revival style Anglican **Christ Church Cathedral** ❼ (tel: 604-682-3484; http://thecathedral. ca; visits: Mon–Fri 10am–4pm; services: Sun 10.30am and 5.30pm), completed in 1895, looks unassuming from the outside, but it's worth going in to see the city's oldest church, with its beautiful stained glass and checkerboard floor.

The Seawall

The 28km waterfront path has clearly marked lanes to separate walkers and runners from cyclists and inline skaters. You can follow the coast around Stanley Park, before the path continues to Spanish Banks Park out to the west. If you would rather cycle, there are bike rental stores at Burrard Landing.

Bill Reid

Bill Reid (1920–98) was born in Victoria and became one of Canada's best-known Indigenous artists and master craftsmen. He was also a broadcaster, a writer, and a prominent First Nations spokesman. Illustrations of his Raven and the First Men, Mythic Messengers, Xhuwaji/Haida Grizzly Bear, and Spirit of Haida Gwaii sculptures are featured on the back of the Canadian $20 dollar bill and he has been honoured with a series of Canada Post stamps.

Vancouver Art Gallery

VANCOUVER ART GALLERY

Head back along West Georgia Street to Hornby Street and turn right to the **Vancouver Art Gallery** ⑧ (tel: 604-662-4719; www.vanartgallery.bc.ca; 10am–5pm Mon, Wed, Thu, Sat & Sun, noon–8pm Tue & Fri; tours available). With a reputation for innovative contemporary art, this splendid gallery contains over 11,000 works, featuring British Columbia and Indigenous artists. The gallery also hosts a lively program of events.

VANCOUVER CENTRAL LIBRARY

From **Robson Square** ⑨, which often has events like open-air film screenings and live music, there is great shopping to be done along Robson Street. End this route at the pleasant rooftop garden on top of the **Vancouver Central Library** ⑩ (tel: 604-331-3603; www.vpl.ca/garden) on the block between Homer and Hamilton streets. A few steps away you will find Café Medina, an excellent Downtown brunch, lunch or coffee stop, see ④.

Food and Drink

① COAL HARBOUR CAFÉ

Vancouver Convention Centre; tel: 604-647-7270; daily B and L; $
This place in the East Building of the Vancouver Convention Centre has a fabulous view, although it may occasionally be blocked to some extent by a cruise ship in dock. There's a patio terrace (with heaters) too – perfect for a coffee and a pastry.

② BELLAGGIO CAFÉ

1055 Canada Place, Suite 26; tel: 604-647-7523; www.bellaggio.cafe; daily B, L, and D; $$
A family-run place, where well-presented food comes in generous portions and with efficient service and a good view. Eat inside or on the terrace. The menu includes breakfasts, seafood, pasta, pizza, and vegetarian options.

③ MAHONY & SONS

Burrard Landing, 1055 Canada Place; tel: 604-647-7513; www.discovermahony.com; daily L and D; $$
There's a good and varied menu of appetizers, soups, salads, burgers, tacos, and mains such as fish and chips and seafood chowder. Take-out is available and they have a large, heated patio.

④ CAFÉ MEDINA

780 Richards Street; tel: 604-879-3114; www.medinacafe.com; daily B and L; $$
Quite simply one of the best (and busiest) brunch spots in town, with Mediterranean-inspired cuisine and delicious freshly-baked Belgian waffles. Menu highlights include the salmon fumé ciabatta sandwich with eggs and avocado, lavender latte, and waffles.

Plenty of choice in Chinatown

CHINATOWN AND GASTOWN

Vancouver's two most historic areas are explored here: North America's second-largest Chinatown (after San Francisco) and the even older Gastown neighborhood, which grew from a bar serving loggers, fur-trappers, and other early pioneers, into a town.

DISTANCE: 1.8km (1 mile)
TIME: 2 hours
START: Dr Sun Yat-Sen Classical Chinese Garden
END: Gastown Steam Clock
POINTS TO NOTE: If using public transportation, head for Stadium-Chinatown station. It is wise to stick to the route specified for the Chinatown section. At the time of writing, some of the streets, in addition to Andy Livingstone Park, were best avoided. That said, the route we have chosen should present no safety concerns. Complementary jasmine tea is offered at the Chinese garden, but it is not permitted to bring your own food; also prohibited are smoking, feeding or touching the fish, entering the water features, and climbing the rock mountain.

CHINATOWN

One of the most colourful and fascinating areas in the city, this is a living and working neighborhood catering to Vancouver's large Chinese community. It's full of people going about their day-to-day business, which boosts its charm.

Chinatown faces some big challenges. Historically a low-income neighborhood, it finds itself at the heart of an increasingly expensive city, and predatory real-estate developers are eying it for transformation. To preserve its identity, the Chinatown Revitalization Committee is working to solve the dual issues of gentrification and poverty. Already a National Historic Site of Canada, an application is being made to Unesco for it to also become a World Heritage Site.

DR SUN YAT-SEN CLASSICAL CHINESE GARDEN

From Stadium Chinatown station, exit beneath the overpass onto Expo Boulevard and follow the curve to the left for a short distance before turning left onto Abbot Street. At the crossroads, go right onto Keefer Street and continue for three blocks, with Andy Livingstone Park to your right (do not go into the park). The entrance to the garden is at Keefer and Carrall streets.

Dr Sun Yat-Sen Park, an oasis of tranquility in busy Vancouver

The first authentic Chinese garden to be established outside of China, the **Dr Sun Yat-Sen Classical Chinese Garden** ❶ (578 Carrall Street; http://vancouver chinesegarden.com; mid-Jun–Aug daily 9.30am–7pm, May–mid-Jun and Sep daily 10am–6pm, Oct daily 10am–4.30pm, Nov–Apr Tue–Sun 10am–4.30pm) opened here in 1986, a peaceful haven in this busy city. The garden experience can be greatly enhanced by taking a 45-minute tour (reservations not necessary), in which the docent will interpret the significance of the design features

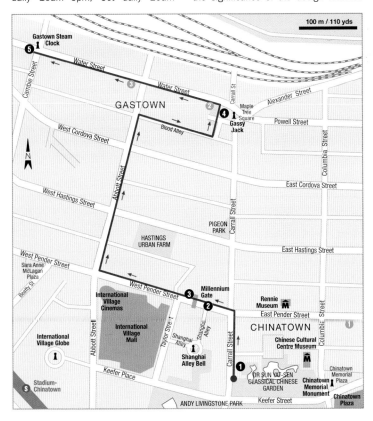

Millennium Gate

and impart historical information about the garden and Chinatown. The shop here sells local art and crafts, from which the profits go to fund cultural programs. The garden has an artist-in-residence program and hosts various events.

It would be wrong to visit Chinatown and not eat there, so after leaving the garden, detour right on East Pender Street to **Chinatown BBQ**, see ①. Afterward, return along East Pender Street, crossing Carrall Street onto West Pender Street. If you are skipping the meal, exit the garden turning right on Carrall Street and when you reach the Pender Street intersection, turn left.

WEST PENDER STREET AND THE MILLENNIUM GATE

One of the most interesting buildings on **West Pender Street ②**, at No. 8, on the left around the corner from Carrall Street, is the Sam Kee Building and its quirky overhanging upper storey. Officially this is the shallowest commercial building in the world. After purchasing the building lot in 1912, the owners were dismayed when the city widened the street and reduced their surface area to only 1.5 metres (less than 5ft) deep. Undeterred, they built on it in 1913 anyway, with a lower level that extends beneath the road.

A little further along, you can't miss the **Millennium Gate ③** – a tall and colourful three-section archway spanning the road, topped by three traditional Chinese-style tiled roofs and flanked with Chinese inscriptions. This grand, inviting beacon marks the site where Chinatown was first established.

GASSY JACK STATUE

Continue along Pender Street West, passing on the left another entrance to the International Village Mall, then at Abbott Street, turn right. Cross both West Hastings Street and West Cordova Street, then look for narrow Blood Alley on the right. Follow this and then go left on Carrall Street to reach the 6-metre (20ft) high bronze statue of **Gassy Jack ④** on Maple Tree Square, at the corner of Water Street. The work of BC artist Vern Simpson in 1970, it marks the spot where Gassy Jack established the saloon from which Vancouver grew.

> ## Gassy Jack
>
> John Deighton, from the town of Hull in northern England, was variously a sailor, a gold prospector, and a bar owner. Among his contemporaries, though, he was best known as a talker, which earned him his 'gassy' nickname. As the first settler on this spot, it was after him that Gastown was named. He had immediately recognized the great potential of the location, predicting that it would one day become a great port. He later built a hotel, the Deighton (lost to a fire in 1886) at the corner of what are now Water and Carrall streets. His statue marks the spot.

Gastown Steam Clock

Appropriately, Jack stands atop a whisky barrel.

GASTOWN STEAM CLOCK

Turn left onto Water Street, lined with trees and restaurants; **MeeT**, see ②, for vegans and the **Flying Pig**, see ③, for meat-eaters are good places to refuel.

At Cambie Street, glance to the right for a view between the buildings of the harbour, then turn your attention to the **Gastown Steam Clock** ⑤ that stands on the corner. This remarkable Edwardian-style timepiece was built in 1977 by master horologist Raymond Saunders, and has fascinated pedestrians ever since.

Its location on top of a steam vent was deliberate; the steam doesn't actually power the clock but it does operate the four pipes that turn out a rather breathy version of the Westminster chimes tune, and then marks the hour by shooting steam upward through a fifth pipe on top of the clock. If you are wondering how this complex contraption can possibly keep time, here's the secret: it does its best, and then an electric backup ensures that complete accuracy is maintained.

Continue along Water Street, with the Vancouver Lookout (see page 28) coming into view ahead. At the end of Water Street, go right on West Cordova Street, and Waterfront Station is on the right.

Food and Drink

① CHINATOWN BBQ

130 East Pender Street; tel: 604-428-2626; Tue–Sun L and early D; $
It may not be fancy – in fact it is decidedly 'no-frills' – but they really know how to do authentic Cantonese barbecue here, and a good menu of crispy pork, poached chicken with ginger scallion sauce, BBQ duck, and curried beef brisket is on offer. Sides for the brave include jellyfish marinated in sesame and chili, and soy sauce chicken feet – but there are plenty of other choices!

② MEET

12 Water Street (inner courtyard, or access via Blood Alley); tel: 604-696-1111;
www.meetonmain.com; daily L and D; $$
Non-vegans love this place too, but if you are vegan, you'll appreciate the amount of choice, including eight types of burgers, bowl food, salads, and delicious desserts. Much of what's on offer is gluten-free too. There's a good range of wines and craft cocktails. If they are busy they'll text you when your table is ready.

③ THE FLYING PIG

102 Water Street; tel: 604-559-7968;
theflyingpigvan.com; daily L and D; $$$
Not a pork restaurant by any means. You'll find a good selection of steaks, seafood, and chicken on the menu – but, for a truly Canadian experience, add a side of the pulled-pork poutine (fries topped with cheese curds and gravy).

The homage to Terry Fox

YALETOWN AND GRANVILLE ISLAND

This walk will appeal to sports, food, and arts fans alike – plus children will love the ferry ride over to Granville Island. Yaletown is full of boutiques and restaurants, and shares a similar industrial history with Granville Island.

DISTANCE: 4.5km (2.8 miles), plus ferry ride
TIME: One day
START: BC Place
END: Granville Island Ferry Dock
POINTS TO NOTE: The nearest Skytrain station to the start point is Stadium/Chinatown; from here you can either go up the stairs to Beatty Street and turn left or go down stairs to Expo Boulevard and go right. Both options are a five-minute walk. If you're driving, there is a handy parking lot off Pacific Boulevard behind the stadium. Do not consider driving to Granville Island – parking is limited, none of it is free, and the narrow streets are congested. Ferries span False Creek and operate almost continuously to Granville Island. The Public Market and Net Loft are closed on Mondays in January and on some public holidays, and the farmers' market only operates on summer Thursdays. If you plan to shop at the Public Market, bring a reusable shopping bag – the market is zero waste and has banned plastic bags.

TERRY FOX STATUE

Not one, but four bronze images of **Terry Fox** ❶ look down the length of Robson Street. This work by Douglas Coupland pays tribute to a young man who died well before his time, and who remained beloved by all Canadians (see page 40).

BC PLACE

Sports fans will find much to engage them in BC's biggest arena, **BC Place** ❷ (tel: 604-669-2300; http://bcplace.com; http://bcsportshall.com). Options for those who love sport include checking out the fascinating BC Sports Hall of Fame – which charts the history of sport in the province from Indigenous sports right through to the Winter Olympics of 2010 – or taking a guided tour (tel: 604-687-5520 for reservations). Of course, you coul also attend a game; the arena plays host to the BC Lions (football), Vancouver Whitecaps (soccer), and Canada Sevens (rugby) – so choose your favourite sport and book tickets early!

YALETOWN

Walk through the **Plaza of Nations ⑤**, built for Expo 86, and follow the seawall past the manicured lawns of Coopers Park and the Quayside Marina. From here, cross Pacific Boulevard and head into charming, low-rise **Yaletown ④**. This neighborhood has come a long way since its former incarnation as an industrial area and railroad terminal. It's now filled with trendy boutiques and artsy places to eat and drink.

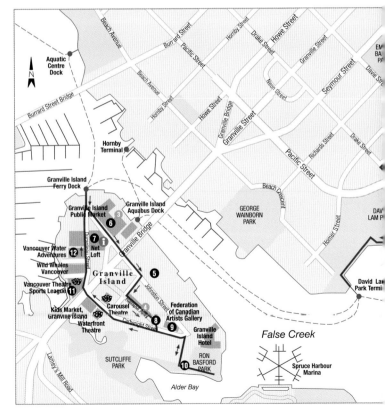

The view towards Yaletown

The former railway engine shed is now the Roundhouse Community Arts & Recreation Centre and still houses a historic steam locomotive. Yaletown is a pleasant place for a stroll and a bite to eat; try the **Distillery Bar & Kitchen**, see ❶, for its patio or convivial pub inside, or the **Blue Water Café**, see ❷, for sophisticated fine dining. The Roundhouse is roughly the same distance from either the Yaletown dock or the David Lam Park dock, but it's a faster ferry ride to the island from David Lam Park (enter via the pathway at

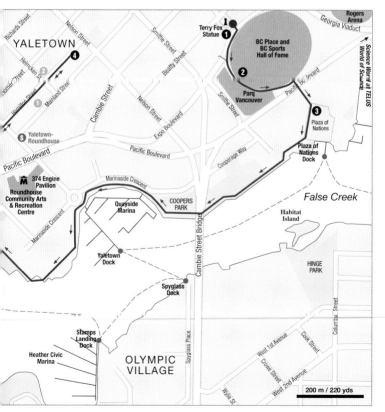

An aerial view of Granville Island

the corner of Drake Street and Pacific Boulevard and follow it to the waterside where it meets the sea wall heading south toward the ferry terminal).

GRANVILLE ISLAND

From either the Aquabus dock or False Creek Ferries dock (both land at the northeast end of **Granville Island ❺**) you'll see signposts announcing the public market. Head in that direction; follow the signs, and enter the market. If you haven't yet had breakfast, you should make a beeline for **Market Grill**, see ❸.

The complete redevelopment of what was a formerly post-industrial wasteland has turned Granville Island into a bustling working neighborhood

populated by an interesting melange of people. It's not far to walk from one end to the other, but there is so much to see and do along the way that it could easily occupy a whole day if you have time to spend.

THE PUBLIC MARKET

The real star of the show here is the **Granville Island Public Market ❻** (http://granvilleisland.com; public market daily 9am–6pm, except Mon in Jan; farmers' market early June–late Sep Thu 10am–3pm). It houses more than 50 vendors selling day-to-day items and specialty foods, much of it produced right here on the doorstep in Vancouver, while other produce is imported, and some of the market's offerings – like the yummy cardamom ganache at ChocolaTas – is only available here. Artisan cheeses and pickles, unusual teas, organic fruit and vegetables, ethical meats, and all kinds of sweet treats will have your mouth watering as you wander the aisles and chat with the vendors. A fantastic tip is to put together a picnic from the delicious odds and ends you can find here, and enjoy it later on in Ron Basford Park.

It's not all about food in the market, though it does steal the limelight! There are also tables rented by artists and artisans to display their wares where you're likely find that perfect souvenir or gift, either for a loved one or just for you.

Terry Fox

Canadians from coast to coast revere the name Terry Fox. At 18 he lost most of his right leg to cancer, but resolved to run across Canada to raise awareness and money for cancer research. He set out on his 'Marathon of Hope' from Newfoundland in April 1980 and ran for 143 days, covering 5,373km (3,339 miles). Only when the cancer spread to his lungs did the young hero reluctantly give up. He died in June 1981 at the age of 22, but some 900 Terry Fox runs still take place all over Canada each fall.

The Public Market, the hub of Granville Island

NET LOFT AND RAILSPUR ALLEY

As you leave the Public Market and head out onto Johnston Street, the **Net Loft** ❼ will be almost opposite you. The Net Loft houses a selection of boutiques showcasing unique Vancouver designers and craftspeople where you can buy unusual beads with which to make your own necklaces and jewelry, find eco-friendly products, or pick up hand-made garments.

Continue on Johnston Street, then go right onto Old Bridge Street. **Railspur Alley** ❽ will be a little way down on your left, with the white building of the Liberty Distillery (www.theliberty distillery.com; 11am–9pm daily, happy hour 3–6pm Mon–Thu and after 8pm nightly; tours at 11.30am and 1.30pm Sat & Sun; reservations recommended tel: 604-558-1998) on the corner. The distillery turns out hand-crafted whiskey, gin, and vodka, and there's a old-fashioned cocktail lounge on sit. Distillery tours are available, and it's well worth taking one for an insight into how distilleries function. Continuing down the alley, murals brighten up some otherwise bleak concrete industrial leftovers and performance artists and musicians often take to the streets, entertaining passers-by. There are places to eat here too, some with outdoor seating if the weather permits. If by now you've walked off the samples from the Public Market, make a stop off for lunch at **Off the Tracks Espresso Bar and Bistro**, see ❹.

FEDERATION OF CANADIAN ARTISTS GALLERY

Continue to the end of Railspur Alley, then go left on Cartwright Street. In a bright, turquoise-coloured building on the corner, the superb **Federation of Canadian Artists Gallery** ❾ (tel: 604-681-8534; http://artists.ca; Tue–Sat 10am–4pm, Sun 10am–3pm) has been supporting and showcasing Canadian artists for nearly 80 years. There's always something interesting and thought-provoking to be seen here, with two exhibitions every month and three major shows a year.

RON BASFORD PARK

Exiting the Federation of Canadian Artists Gallery, you will see greenery ahead; head that way, perhaps with some picnic supplies. At the southeastern tip of the island, **Ron Basford Park** ❿ is a lovely haven and makes for a nice place to relax. At its heart is a hill from the summit of which you can enjoy a stunning view across the island.

CARTWRIGHT AND DURANLEAU STREETS

On leaving Ron Basford Park, backtrack on Johnston Street for a short distance,

Crowds enjoying the sunshine on Granville Island

then branch left on Cartwright Street. This will give you a round-trip back to the ferry, with more galleries and shops along your way back.

After passing under the bridge, branch right on Anderson Street and then join Duranleau Street. The Improv Centre comedy venue, home to the **Vancouver Theatre Sports League** ⓫, is on your left. Later, a series of side streets lead to more boutiques and operators offering whale-watching cruises. Farther along Duranleau, another street to the left is home to **Van-couver Water Adventures** ⓬ (1812 Boatlift Lane; tel: 604-736-5155; www.vancouverwateradventures.com) providing high-speed Zodiac tours as well as kayak, paddleboard, and Seadoo rentals. Duranleau Street soon brings you back to the Granville Island Public Market, where you can head back to the ferry or circle round to Johnston Street again to see whether the Arts Club Theatre Company have anything on at the Granville Island Stage (1585 Johnston Street; tel: 604-687-1644; www.artsclub.com).

Food and Drink

① DISTILLERY BAR & KITCHEN

1131 Mainland Street, Yaletown; tel: 604-669-2255; http://mjg.ca/distillery-bar-and-kitchen; Wed–Fri D, Sat & Sun B, L, and D; $$

With two heated patios, this is a great place to sit outside and watch the world go by. The food is made-from-scratch Italian-American, and there's a good range of cocktails.

② BLUE WATER CAFÉ

1095 Hamilton Street, Yaletown; tel: 604-688-8078; www.bluewatercafe.net; daily D; $$$$

Upscale restaurant specializing in responsibly caught or sustainably farmed local seafood and top quality beef and chicken (and a huge range of oysters) in elegant surroundings.

③ MARKET GRILL

104–1689 Johnston Street, Granville Island; tel: 604-689-1918; daily B, L and early D; $$

Whether you want a big plate of bacon and eggs or a quick breakfast sandwich, this is a great place to fuel up for the day. Or come back later and check out the full menu: the burgers – beef, salmon, chicken, or veggie – are highly recommended.

④ OFF THE TRACKS ESPRESSO BAR AND BISTRO

1363 Railspur Alley, Granville Island; tel: 604-689-8700; www.tracksbistro.ca; daily B & L; $

A stylish place, with outdoor seating and an upstairs room with board games. Coffee is locally roasted and the food comes from local organic sources. There's all-day breakfast, soups, salads and sandwiches, plus local craft beers. Check out the vintage espresso machine.

Traditional totem Poles in Satnley Park

STANLEY PARK

One of the main attractions in the city is to the northwest of the downtown area. This vast, lovely park occupies a peninsula that's almost completely encircled by the waters of the Burrard Inlet; the Vancouver Seawall hugs the coast all the way round.

DISTANCE: 5km (3 miles)

TIME: One day

START: Vancouver Aquarium

END: Vancouver Aquarium

POINTS TO NOTE: You can get to the park on public transportation (bus 19), but there's none around the park, though you can take a 15-minute ride on the Stanley Park Train or a horse-drawn carriage tour. If driving, enter the park at the west end of Georgia Street. From there, Stanley Park Drive encircles the park, with Avison Way cutting across via the Vancouver Aquarium. Route 99 (aka Stanley Park Causeway) bisects the park on its way to the Lions Gate Bridge and the North Shore. Drivers will find plenty of places to park; the daily pass lets you re-park at a number of parking places around the park. It's less than a half-hour's walk on the Seawall from its beginning at Burrard Landing to the park, or you could rent bicycles at Canada Place. You can get express entry to the Vancouver Aquarium by buying tickets online or by paying with a credit card on arrival.

This walk explores a Vancouver highlight, Stanley Park. There is an information center and bicycles available for hire from Spokes Bicycle Rentals (tel: 604-688-5141; spokesbicyclerentals.com) at the entrance.

Within Stanley Park's 405 hectares (1,000 acres) there are a couple of lovely beaches, the largest aquarium in Canada, traditional totem poles, historical landmarks, a miniature railway, and half a million trees. This land was the traditional territory of Coast Salish peoples but today it bears the same name as the coveted Stanley Cup (for hockey), both named after former Governor General, Lord Frederick Stanley (1841–1908).

VANCOUVER AQUARIUM

Set aside a couple of hours to explore the excellent **Vancouver Aquarium ❶** (845 Avison Way; infoline: 604-659-3474 or tel: 604-659-3400; www.vanaqua.org; daily 10am–5pm, closes at 4pm some public holidays), featuring some 50,000 marine creatures. Before you enter, admire the splendid Chief of the Under-

Sea lions at Vancouver Aquarium

sea World sculpture, designed by Indigenous artist Bill Reid (see page 31).

The Pacific Coast and Canadian Arctic are well represented in the aquarium, including a huge exhibit on the marine life of the Strait of Georgia. There are tropical species of all shapes, sizes and colours, including underwater dwellers, amphibians, and dry-land creatures such as snakes, spiders, monkeys, and birds.

Admission includes a show in the 4-D theater, offering an immersive experience with sights, sounds, movement, aromas, and even weather conditions associated with what's on screen. There are also opportunities for behind-the-scenes tours to see the work of the staff and throughout the day there are special events, including shark feeding, sea lion training, and the chance to meet a tortoise. Doing its bit for the plastics problem, the aquarium doesn't sell bottled water; instead, it provides stations where you can refill your own bottle.

If you are here in June–September when it is open, have a bite to eat in the **Ocean Wise Café**, see ❶, beside the entrance.

TOTEM POLES

From the aquarium, go down Avison Way toward the information booth, then go left onto the **Seawall ❷**, with masses of boats moored offshore. Continue around the Seawall for a view of the Royal Canadian Navy Reserve's HMCS Discovery shore base, named after George Vancou-

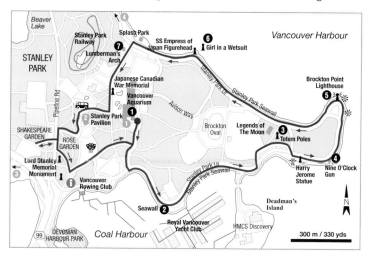

Nine O'Clock Gun   *Lumberman's Arch*

ver's vessel (see page 11), over on the evocatively named Deadman's Island.

A little further, near Brockton Point, is one of the most popular sights in Stanley Park, the **Totem Poles ❸**, found within a group of trees to the left. This collection of nine totem poles was created by artists from three of the Indigenous peoples of the Pacific Coast: Haida Gwaii, Rivers Inlet, and Squamish. Some are now replicas, the originals either housed in museums for preservation or, in the case of the Skedans Mortuary Pole, returned to the originating nation, the Haida Gwaii.

NINE O'CLOCK GUN AND THE LIGHTHOUSE

Go back to the Seawall and turn left to continue the way you were going until you reach the **Nine O'Clock Gun ❹**. If you want to witness the firing of this historic naval cannon, you need to be here at 9pm. It's hard to get a definitive explanation about why it was placed here – it was made in England in 1816 and brought here in 1894. It was never fired in anger, but it seems to have acted as a timepiece. If you're out of earshot at 9pm, you can follow the gun on Twitter – you'll receive a "boom" daily at 9pm Pacific Time.

Continuing around the Seawall, you'll soon come to the sturdy little **Brockton Point Lighthouse ❺**. There's been a lighthouse here since 1890, although the current red-and-white striped building dates from 1914, and the light is only occasionally switched on. It's a pictur-

esque spot, with a distant view across the water of North Shore buildings and the hills behind.

FEMALE FIGURES

Looping around the headland on the Seawall, and passing the Totem Poles again on their opposite side, you'll come to the **Girl in a Wetsuit ❻** just offshore. A plaque on the Seawall states that the statue, unveiled in 1972, represents the city's dependence on the sea. Nearby is a replica of the colourful Empress of Japan figurehead (the original is in the Maritime Museum, see page 70), which fronted its ship across the Pacific Ocean more than 400 times.

LUMBERMAN'S ARCH

Continuing on the Seawall, you'll soon find yourself close to the aquarium again, down the road to your left, but continue a little farther and, just after passing the Fox's Den Splash Park on the right – where you'll probably spend some time if you've got children with you – head left to the huge chunks of tree trunks that make up the **Lumberman's Arch ❼**, which honors the occupation that helped to shape the history of British Columbia. From here wander at will, seeking out the various gardens that lie sheltered among the trees to the west of the aquarium: the Rock Garden, Rose Garden, Air Force Garden of Remembrance, and Shakespeare Garden. **Stanley's Bar and Grill**, see ❶,

Third Beach is a great place to relax in the late afternoon

overlooking the Rose Garden, is a good place to eat. Farther west from the latter, at the site of the Vancouver Miniature Railway, is another superb work of Indigenous art, Raven: Spirit of Transformation, created from a piece of wood felled by a catastrophic windstorm in 2006.

Explore the trails that lead through the park's wooded areas or relax on one of the beaches. Third Beach, on the western edge of the park, has a long stretch of sand and the famous **Teahouse Restaurant**, see ③, where you can grab a bite to eat. Another eating option is the **Prospect Point Bar, Grill and Café**, see ④, up near the Lions Gate Bridge. There are opportunities for bird- and wild-life-watching at the Lost Lagoon or Beaver Lake, or you could hop aboard the carriage of Stanley Park Horse-Drawn Tours (tel: 604-681-5115; Mar–Nov 22), which depart from the kiosk in the Coal Harbour parking lot. Reservations are not required. If there's something on at the Malkin Bowl, it might be worth sticking around into the evening; it hosts Theatre under the Stars events in summer and occasional big-name concerts.

Food and Drink

① OCEAN WISE (WATERFALL) CAFÉ
June–Sep, daily L and D; $$
Next to the aquarium entrance (you don't need to be an aquarium visitor), overlooking Bill Reid's Undersea World sculpture, this restaurant is run by executive chef Ned Bell, a well-known and award-winning advocate for sustainable seafood.

② STANLEY'S BAR AND GRILL
Stanley Park Pavilion; 610 Pipeline Road; tel: 604-602-3088; http://stanleyparkpavilion.com; daily L and early D; $$
In a lovely historic building fronted by the beautiful Stanley Park Rose Garden, the grill serves soups, salads, classic burgers, and mains that might include pasta, curry, and grilled salmon. Ingredients are local and healthy.

③ THE TEAHOUSE RESTAURANT
Ferguson Point, Stanley Park; tel: 604-669-3281; daily L and D; $$$
Contemporary restaurant overlooking English Bay and the North Shore. The lunch menu features pizzas, burgers (beef or salmon), omelettes, and sandwiches, while at dinner there might be sablefish, rack of lamb, duck confit, and steaks.

④ PROSPECT POINT BAR, GRILL & CAFÉ
5601 Stanley Park Drive; tel: 604-669-2737; http://prospectpoint.com; daily L and D (ice cream available until 6pm); $$
The large outdoor deck here has a great view of the Lions Gate Bridge. The bar and grill serves up pub-style fare that includes vegetarian and seafood choices, and on the drinks menu you'll find craft beers and sangria; the café has locally roasted coffee, baked goods and ice cream.

Gardens at UBC

UNIVERSITY OF BRITISH COLUMBIA

This is one of the most scenic and 'greenest' university campuses anywhere, where you'll find excellent museums, an art gallery, several beautiful gardens, a sustainability research farm, and even, perhaps, a concert or play to end the day.

DISTANCE: 5km (3 miles)
TIME: A full day
START: Museum of Anthropology
END: UBC Botanical Garden
POINTS TO NOTE: Nearly a dozen city buses serve the UBC Exchange, but 49 is probably the best option – get off at the UBC Exchange for the start of the walk, then pick it up from the stop on W 16th Avenue at the end of the walk. There are two shuttle buses (68 and 70) that circle the campus from UBC Exchange. If driving, take 4th, 10th or 16th Avenue West; there are plenty of parking lots on campus (www.parking. ubc.ca). The Beaty Biodiversity Museum is closed Mondays and and the Museum of Anthropology is closed Mondays from mid-October to mid-May. The UBC Museums Pass will save you money on the combined admission fees for the two museums and also gives a 10 percent discount in both museum shops; every third Thursday of the month, admission to the Beaty is by donation from 5–8.30pm.

On the headland bordering the south side of the Burrard Inlet, the Vancouver campus of the University of British Columbia looks toward snow-capped mountains.

MUSEUM OF ANTHROPOLOGY

Go west along Chancellor Boulevard onto NW Marine Drive; at the intersection with West Mall, you'll find the MOA on the right. The **Museum of Anthropology** ❶ (6393 NW Marine Drive; http://moa.ubc.ca; mid-May–mid-Oct daily 10am–5pm, mid-Oct–mid-May Tue–Sun 10am–5pm) mainly focusses on British Columbia's First Nations; the Great Hall displays a superb collection of totems and collections from other parts of the world range from Latvian ceramics to Japanese woodblock prints. The **Café MOA**, see ❶, is perfect for a bite to eat.

MORRIS AND HELEN BELKIN ART GALLERY

From the museum, exit onto NW Marine Drive going right, then turn left on West Mall, at Crescent Road, turn left and con-

The Anthropology Museum i

tinue to reach an open area with a flagpole in the centre. Turn right onto Main Mall, and the **Morris and Helen Belkin Gallery ❷** (1825 Main Mall; www.belkin.ubc.ca; Tue–Sun 10am–5pm during exhibitions) will be on your right. This modern space mounts at least four exhibitions a year.

NITOBE MEMORIAL GARDEN

Retrace your steps down Crescent Road and along West Mall; at Memorial Rd turn right and continue to the **Nitobe Memorial Garden ❸** (https://botanicalgarden.ubc.ca/visit/nitobe-memorial-garden; Wed–Sun 10am–3pm; possibly longer hours in summer, check ahead). The garden is among the top five Japanese gardens outside of Japan. Features include spritually significant lanterns and figures, a classical tea house, where visitors can experience a traditional tea ceremony (May–Sep; additional fee), and a statue of Dr. Inazo

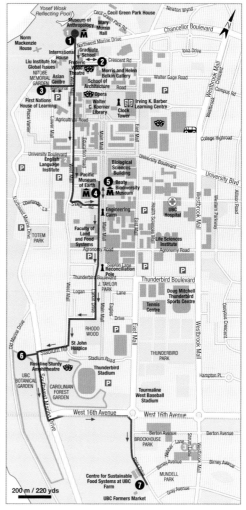

Nitobe Memorial Garden
Campus building at UBC

Nitobe, the Japanese statesman, philosopher and scholar who devoted himself to promoting cross-Pacific relations.

PACIFIC MUSEUM OF EARTH

From the Nitobe Garden exit, at the crosswalk turn left up Memorial Road, then go right on West Mall. After crossing University Boulevard, **Mercante**, see ②, is on the right. Continue until Stores Road, where you turn left to reach the **Pacific Museum of Earth ❹** (6339 Stores Road; https://pme.ubc.ca; Mon–Fri 10am–5pm). Fascinating displays on the geology and evolution of our planet, including engaging interactive exhibits such as a tornado machine, an OmniGlobe that projects all kinds of stunning images, and a green screen where visitors can play a TV weather person.

The Green University

The University of British Columbia's Vancouver campus is committed to sustainability and environmental issues. Many of the buildings have been provided with energy-saving and other 'green' features, and instructive guided tours are offered (http://sustain.ubc.ca/tours); for a self-guided tour, download the 'sustainable campus walking tour map'. Part of the university's Centre for Interactive Research on Sustainability (CIRS) is open to the public, in addition to the Centre for Sustainable Food Systems at UBC Farm.

BEATY BIODIVERSITY MUSEUM

Continue along Stores Road to the Main Mall. Turn left and the museum is a short distance along on the right. The **Beaty Biodiversity Museum ❺** (2212 Main Mall; http://beatymuseum.ubc.ca; Tue–Sun 10am–5pm, Thu until 8.30pm) is UBC's natural history museum, which boasts a huge blue whale skeleton – the largest in Canada – as well as dinosaur footprints.

UBC BOTANICAL GARDEN

From the Beaty, it's a 15-minute walk south along Main Mall, turning right at Thunderbird Boulevard, left at Larkin Drive, then veering southwest toward SW Marine Drive (cross at the pedestrian crossing extending from Stadium Road) to the entrance to the **UBC Botanical Garden ❻** (http://botanicalgarden.ubc.ca; Wed–Sun 10am–3pm; longer hours in summer, check ahead). This is Canada's oldest botanical garden, which celebrated its centenary in 2016. Extending to 23.5 hectares (58 acres), it features themed areas including the BC Rainforest Garden, replicating the plants and microclimate of the province's coastal regions, and the Carolinian Forest Garden, representing a small area in Ontario that contains more than half Canada's native trees. Flower gardens include one featuring Alpine plants, an Asian garden, a physic garden with medicinal plants and woodland garden, as well as a sustainable food garden

with vegetables, herbs, and fruits. There's also information on eco-friendly gardening and the Greenheart TreeWalk, where visitors can explore suspended walkways. Free guided tours are available; reserve your spot as soon as you arrive.

CENTRE FOR SUSTAINABLE FOOD SYSTEMS AT UBC FARM

Some parts of the Botanical Garden, including the Food Garden, are across the road from the main entrance at the corner of SW Marine Drive and W 16th Avenue; end your visit to the garden here. A path here leads out to W 16th, where you should go left as far as the traffic circle, but cross over just before it at the pedestrian crossings, then round the corner onto Ross Drive to find the entrance to the **Centre for Sustainable Food Systems at UBC Farm** ❼ (3461 Ross Drive; http://ubcfarm.ubc.ca; Mar–Oct Mon–Sat 9am–5pm, Nov–Mar Mon–Fri 9am–5pm). At 24 hectares (60 acres) of farmland and forest, the center is dedicated to research into sustainable food production. It hosts a bustling farmers' market on Saturdays from late June to mid-Oct, and the farm also supplies the university's food outlets. Nearby options to feast on the farm's tasty homegrown produce include **Virtuous Pie**, see ❸, or **Biercraft**, see ❹, both on Shrum Lane.

Food and Drink

❶ CAFÉ MOA
6393 NW Marine Drive; tel: 604-827-4738; Tue–Sun L; $
The café in the Museum of Anthropology serves sandwiches, pastries, hot food, and vegetarian options.

❷ MERCANTE
6488 University Boulevard; tel: 604-827-2210; www.food.ubc.ca/place/mercante; Mon–Fri B, L and D, Sat–Sun L and D; $
This is a cozy, informal place serving authentic Italian food. Made-to-order pizzas are straight from the hot-stone hearth oven, and there are also breakfasts (except weekends), pasta dishes, salads, and specialty coffees.

❸ VIRTUOUS PIE
3339 Shrum Lane, Westbrook Village; tel: 604-428-1060; virtuouspie.com; daily L and D; $
All the food here is plant-based – even the 'meatballs' – and includes hand-crafted pizzas made with nut-based cheeses and three-day dough, salads, and artisan ice cream.

❹ BIERCRAFT
3340 Shrum Lane, Westbrook Village; tel: 604-559-2437; www.biercraft.com; daily L and D; $$
One of three locations, this Westbrook Village site serves a wide range of craft beers and imported brews from around the world. A long menu of inventive pub food is available for lunch and dinner and there's also weekend brunch and a menu dedicated to mussels.

The Capilano Suspension Bridge

CAPILANO AND GROUSE MOUNTAIN

These two excursions from Vancouver are at the top of most to-do lists, one with an exciting rope bridge across a canyon and a cliff walk, the other a SkyRide cable car ride up to a mountain peak with stunning views and lots to see and do.

DISTANCE: 12km (7.5 miles)
TIME: One day
START: Capilano Suspension Bridge Park
END: Grouse Mountain
POINTS TO NOTE: Grouse Mountain and Capilano Suspension Bridge Park both operate free shuttle buses from Canada Place (near the info kiosk) on a first-come, first-served basis. Admission fees are payable before you get on, but the bus itself is free. Times vary. Capilano's shuttle also picks up at Library Square (at Homer at Robson), Melville Street (at the Hyatt Hotel entrance), and the Blue Horizon Hotel on Robson Street. There is also a service from downtown on bus 246. Alternative public transportation is on bus 232 from Phibbs Exchange, or via the Seabus from Waterfront Station to North Vancouver, then bus 236. If driving, there's a fee for parking at Grouse Mountain. From June to August, arrive before 10am or after 5pm to avoid the crowds at Capilano. Strollers are not allowed on the bridge so babies and toddlers must be carried.

CAPILANO

One of the most popular sights in the greater Vancouver area is the **Capilano Suspension Bridge Park** ❶ (www.cap bridge.com; daily 9am–5pm late Jan–mid Apr and mid-Oct–mid-Nov, 9am–6pm mid-Sep–mid-Oct, 9am–7pm mid-Apr–mid-May and early to mid-Sep, 8am–8pm mid-May–early Sep, 11am–9pm late Nov–late Jan). Built in 1889, the Suspension Bridge spans the deep gorge of the Capilano River, a distance of 137 meters (450ft) at a height of 70 meters (230ft). It is not a rigid structure: you'll feel it swaying slightly as you cross, but millions have crossed safely (a very few foolhardy individuals have not) during its lifetime, and it is a tremendous experience, accompanied by the tantalizing aroma of cedar emanating from the dense rainforest on the other side.

The adventure doesn't stop there. Threading through this ancient forest, and climbing to a height of 33 meters (108ft) into the canopy, is the Treetops Adventure, consisting of seven suspension bridges and viewing platforms

A section of the Cliffwalk at Capilano

ingeniously engineered to preserve and allow continued growth of all the trees to which it is attached. Guided tours explain the rainforest environment.

Not exciting enough for you yet? Then head for the Cliffwalk, a thrilling series of walkways clinging to the cliff face high above the river, some sections with glass floors for the ultimate downward view.

Back on the ground, all this has probably worked up an appetite, and there are various options here. Try the **Cliff House Restaurant**, see ❶, which overlooks the canyon.

To round off the visit, the Story Centre has all kinds of information and displays relating to the history of the bridge, the rainforest and the wildlife of the ecosystem. There are also exhibits on the culture of the First Nations at Kia'palano, including a number of totem poles. The shop is worth checking out too for the Indigenous designs and local specialty foods.

During the Winter Lights Festival, from late November to late January, thousands of lights illuminate all the features of the park, including eight of the living Douglas firs as Christmas trees.

GROUSE MOUNTAIN

Continuing north from Capilano Suspension Bridge Park, it's just under 4km (2.5 miles) to the bottom of **Grouse Mountain** ❷ (6400 Nancy Greene Way, North Vancouver; www.grousemountain.com; daily 9am–9pm).

The trip up to the summit on the Skyride is a great start, with breathtaking views all around, and there's the chance

The exhilarating Skyride up Grouse Mountain

for a few lucky passengers to ride in an open-air enclosure on top of the cabin.

Up at the summit you will find the Grouse Mountain Refuge for Endangered Wildlife, home to grizzly bears and timber wolves. Ranger talks are included in the admission price, and Breakfast with the Bears, which, for an extra fee, includes a ranger talk and then a 'bear-inspired' breakfast in the Grizzly Lookout Café.

Other attractions on offer are a Lumberjack Show, a birds of prey demonstration, and a trip up The Eye of the Wind the only wind turbine in the world with a glass viewing pod right at the top, 58 meters (190ft) above the mountaintop.

Reservations and an additional fee are required for this. Activities include the Mountain Ropes Adventure – an aerial walk in which, safely harnessed, you can negotiate four courses with various degrees of difficulty; there's an easier kids' version too, featuring tree-houses, slides and games. There's also ziplining, paragliding, mountain biking, hiking trails, and, in winter, a full range of winter sports, sleigh rides and Christmas events. For a good introduction to the mountain and its activities, head into the Theatre in the Sky to see the HD movie.

For dinner, choose from **Altitudes Bistro**, see ❷, and **The Observatory**, see ❸.

Food and Drink

❶ CLIFF HOUSE RESTAURANT

Capilano Suspension Bridge Park, 3735 Capilano Road; tel: 604-985-7474; www.capbridge.com; daily L and D; $$$

At the time when the bridge was first built, there was a house on the site of this restaurant and its sturdy wooden beams, antiques and photographs recall those early days. The building has masses of windows to take in the views and there's a patio open in summer. The extensive menu includes Ocean Wise fish and ingredients from local farms. Craft beers, wine, and cocktails are served too.

❷ ALTITUDES BISTRO

Peak Chalet, Grouse Mountain; daily L & D; $$

This casual place, as its name suggests, has incredible views and a great patio. The great fare consists of sharing platters, sandwiches, salads, and main courses such as Portuguese seafood stew, burgers, and vegetarian brown rice buddah bowls.

❸ THE OBSERVATORY

Peak Chalet, Grouse Mountain; tel: 604-998-5045; www.observatoryrestaurant.ca; daily D; $$$$

This is a good place to end the day. It doesn't open until 5pm, and gives you the chance to watch the lights come on across distant Vancouver while enjoying fine, seasonal West Coast cuisine. In addition to the carte, there's a five-course tasting menu. Make a reservation to eat here and it will grant you access to the Skyride and mountain activities.

Sea to Sky Highway – it's all in the name

SEA TO SKY HIGHWAY

This route features the stunningly scenic and aptly named Sea to Sky Highway (officially Highway 99), which hugs the coastline of the Howe Sound then heads up into the mountains to Whistler; in winter, the number one ski resort in North America, and in summer, a world-renowned mountain bike park.

DISTANCE: 121km (75 miles)
TIME: Two days
START: Vancouver
END: Whistler
POINTS TO NOTE: You'll need a car for this route. Be sure to make reservations for an overnight stay (or longer) in Whistler (see page 57). If you want to partake in organized sports or activities in Whistler, arrange this in advance too – the Peak2Peak Experience requires booking three days in advance through the Whistler Visitor Centre or Whistler Blackcomb Guest Relations. Buy tickets for the Sea to Sky Gondola ride online to save money, but make sure you do it more than 12 hours in advance. To gain some background to the Indigenous heritage along the route, download a Cultural Journey Map and related audio from www.slcc.ca/experience/cultural-journey. Check the weather forecast; there is more to this trip than just the views, but they are an important part of it, and fog and low cloud-cover can seriously mar the experience.

Heading out of downtown Vancouver, take the Lion's Gate Bridge from Stanley Park and follow signs for Whistler. Passing through West Vancouver, you'll skirt Horseshoe Bay, with Bowen Island and Hopkins Landing coming into view on the other side of Howe Sound. As you continue north, it won't be not long before the snow-capped mountains come into view, with gorgeous views to the left across the islet-dotted waters of Howe Sound, stretching to the wilderness beyond. To your right, sheer cliffs rise from the edge of the road – be patient and you'll find one or two spots where it's safe to pull over and enjoy it all. Don't be tempted to turn off the highway to look for a viewpoint – side streets are narrow and winding, and residential buildings have got the views all sewn up.

Lion's Bay has a gas station and food should you need it – stay on the highway until you see a blue 'Food' sign with an arrow, then turn off and continue to follow further blue signs that point the way. Rejoin the highway and continue north.

Panning for gold

The copper mine at Brittania Beach

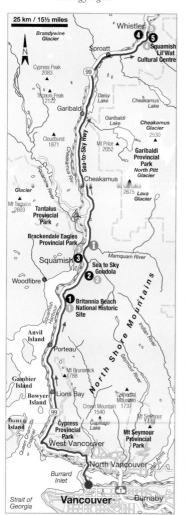

BRITANNIA BEACH NATIONAL HISTORIC SITE

About 50km (30 miles) north of Vancouver, you'll reach **Britannia Beach** ❶, preceded by a pull-off on the right with some information boards. After this you'll pass the industrial buildings of the Britannia Mine Museum (daily 9am–4.30pm early May–mid-Oct, Mon–Fri 10am–4.30pm mid-Oct–end Nov and Feb–early May; www.britanniaminemuseum.ca) on the right

This was the site of the largest copper mine in the British Commonwealth during the 1920s. It ceased operations in the 1970s and was later transformed into a museum. Visitors can visit the old mine site and ride the Underground Train to see live demonstrations. Most of the mine buildings have been preserved as well as the old machinery and processing plant, and the Mine House has three floors of displays. A video relates the history of mining here, and docents dressed as miners are on hand to answer questions.

Another aspect of this site is its use as a movie location. Since the 1990s, countless film shoots have taken place here, including the 1990s TV series *The X-Files* and big-screen hits such as *Star Trek Beyond* (2016), *Insomnia* (2002), *Free Willy 3: The Rescue* (1997), and *Dark Angel* (2000–2002).

The museum has converted one of the historic buildings next to the gift shop into **Chatterbox Cafe**, see ❶.

The viewing platform reached by the Sea to Sky Gondola

Another option is to pick up picnic supplies – just 2km (1 mile) farther north, after passing between high, densely forested rocks on both sides of the road, the Murrin Provincial Park has picnic tables.

SEA TO SKY GONDOLA

Beyond Britannia Beach it begins to feel like you are heading into the sky as the road climbs through a densely forested landscape, but you're not done with the water yet. Rounding a bend to the right, Howe Sound comes back into view and the road descends to run alongside it. Take advantage of the viewpoint on the left here. Soon after comes the Shannon Falls Provincial Park and then, to the

right, the **Sea to Sky Gondola ❷** (www. seatoskygondola.com; daily 10am–6pm mid-May–early Nov, rest of the year daily 10am–4pm, last ride down one hour after last ride up). This ten-minute ride will carry you from near sea-level up to 885 meters (2,903ft). At the top there are three platforms with phenomenal views, a 100-meter (328ft) suspension bridge and various trails; don't miss the Spirit Trail Loop, which tells the story of the Squamish Nation and their relationship to the land. You can enjoy a meal while you take it all in at the **Summit Lodge Restaurant**, see ❼.

SQUAMISH

Continuing north, you'll pass the entrance to the Stawamus Chief Provincial Park on the right, and should take heed of the roadside sign which warns against feeding the bears.

At the north end of Howe Sound, **Squamish ❸** is a good-sized town with all the stores and services you'd expect to find. Stop in at the Adventure Centre (38551 Loggers Lane; www.explore squamish.com) to find out what there is to see and do – outdoor activities are a big draw, and rock climbers, wind-surfers, and mountain bikers are well catered to. You can break your journey here overnight (see page 105).

Squamish is also famous for its over-wintering bald eagles. If you are in this area after early November, you will be treated to the unforgettable sight of

> ### An environmental win
>
> Mining activities at Britannia Beach created catastrophic pollution levels in the Britannia Creek and it wasn't until just after the turn of the 21st century that the problem was addressed. Prior to that the waters, though clear in appearance, were completely dead. Following the plugging of the mine workings and the installation of a water treatment plant, monitoring of the situation has revealed a marked improvement. There is still a way to go, but marine life is returning to the formerly uninhabitable waters. Salmon are spawning here and you may spot orcas and dolphins out in Howe Sound.

Cloudraker Skybridge

their arrival in huge numbers. The main attraction for them is the salmon, which are heading upstream to spawn in the Squamish River. For the eagles' protection, the Brackendale Eagles Provincial Park to the north of Squamish is closed to visitors at this time of year, but there is a viewing shelter with information panels and, on some weekends, interpreters to offer information and high-powered telescopes; from the Sea to Sky Highway, take Depot Road and then Government Road. Eagle-watching rafting trips are available too; for more information visit www.squamishenvironment.ca/programs/eaglewatch.

If you're driving through Squamish, **Zephyr Café**, see ❸, at the centre of town is a laidback place for a healthy bite to eat.

SQUAMISH TO WHISTLER

Continuing north through the strung-out suburbs of Squamish, the road crosses a tributary of the Squamish River, then heads into the Garibaldi Highlands on a tree-lined route. There's a handy viewpoint on the right at the point where the trees break and the high, snow-capped peaks come into view.

The highway continues its steady climb (with a passing lane on the uphill side) between rugged rockfaces; later a picturesque stream flows beside and then under the highway. Soon you'll see Daisy Lake to the right, with the Brandywine Falls Provincial Park wrap-

ping around and extending beyond its northern end. The highway runs through the park, with a short walking trail to the falls off to the right and a vehicle entrance a little farther on. The Welcome to Whistler sign and banners mean that you have nearly reached the town; if you can't wait for the excitement to start, look for the blue sign indicating the Whistler Bungee off to the right.

After passing Alta Lake on the left, signs of habitation appear. Whistler Village is some way ahead, but where you go from here will depend on where you have made reservations for the night.

WHISTLER

Primarily developed a winter-sports resort, **Whistler** ❹ has a great deal to offer year-round, with a long list of organized activities based in and around its purpose-built, traffic-free village, surrounded by spectacular mountain scenery. It started to develop during the 1960s, with an eye on the possibility of one day hosting the Winter Olympic Games, which finally happened in 2010.

One of the highlights is the Peak 2 Peak 360 Experience, which includes a ride in a glass-bottomed gondola between the Whistler and Blackcomb mountain peaks at an altitude of 436 meters (1,427ft), the chance to walk across the Cloudraker Skybridge, a suspension bridge stretching from Whistler Peak to the West Ridge, and the

Cycling in Whistler in spring

Raven's Eye Cliff Walk viewing platform. There are various displays and a film to watch, so allow plenty of time.

Down on the ground, the list of things to do is seemingly endless. Winter sports go without saying, and in summer activities include hiking, mountain biking, taking an off-road 4X4 tour, wild swimming, golf, ziplining, bungee-jumping, and more. There are good wildlife-watching opportunities too, from birds to bears to the marmots that gave Whistler its name (you'll understand when you hear one).

Amid all the outdoorsy aspects of the resort, culture and the arts are not forgotten; Arts Whistler (www.arts whistler.com) has full details of what's on and links to local museums and galleries. Of these, the Whistler Museum has exhibits relating to the town's history and development, and the stunning Audain Art Museum houses a fine collection of British Columbia art and photography, plus around three visiting exhibitions each year. There's a good public library and the Maury Young Arts Centre includes a theater, a youth center, and an art gallery (www. thegallerywhistler.com).

Throughout the year there are festivals and events, great shopping, and a wide range of restaurants and nightlife, from cozy pubs to boisterous nightclubs. For an upscale treat or special occasion dinner, the **Rimrock Café and Oyster Bar**, see ❹, is a good choice.

SQUAMISH LIL'WAT CULTURAL CENTRE

Along the Sea to Sky Highway, you will have noticed some bilingual (Indigenous and English) signage. This reflects the strong Indigenous culture of both the Squamish Nation and the Lil'wat Nation, who have inhabited this region for millennia. An excellent place to learn more is at the **Squamish Lil'Wat Cultural Centre** ❺ (4584 Blackcomb Way; Tue–Sun 10am–5pm) on the edge of Whistler. Inside a stunning modern building, exhibits, performances, and storytelling celebrate their cultures. There are some fine examples of art

Whistler for Families

It goes without saying that children will revel in the activities here. In winter, in addition to skiing and snowboarding, there's a tube park, sleigh and dog-sled rides, and ice-skating. Summer has lots going on for all ages, and year-round there's a tree-top adventure course with ziplines. There are opportunities for parents to get a break from the little ones too, with licensed daycare (tel: 604-905-2496) for young children, activity camps (www.whistlercore.com/pages/camps) for older ones, and babysitting services (www.babysittingwhistler.com). It's also possible to rent baby equipment (www.babysonthego.com), including cribs, strollers, and high chairs.

Snowboarder in Whistler

Squamish Lil'Wat Cultural Centre

and wood-carving, and Cultural Ambassadors from Indigenous Nations give guided tours. Don't miss the **Thunderbird Café**, see ⑤, on the lower level.

The Sea to Sky Highway doesn't end at Whistler, but carries on as far as Pemberton (www.tourismpemberton bc.com), beyond which Highway 99 changes name several times before it ends at Highway 97, just north of the latter's intersection with the TransCanada Highway.

Food and Drink

① CHATTERBOX CAFE

1 Forbes Way, Britannia Beach; tel: 604-896-2233; daily B and L; $

At Britannia Mine (entrance fee not required), this throwback (in name only) to a local 1950s cafe serves freshly-baked treats, plus a range of sandwiches, coffees and specialty teas. Check out the autographed photos from filming here over the years.

② SUMMIT LODGE RESTAURANT

36800 Highway 99, Sea to Sky Gondola Lodge, Squamish; tel: 604-892-2551; www.seatoskygondola.com/facilities/food-beverage; daily L; $$

This is a casual self-service spot with big windows and a deck from which to enjoy the fabulous view. There's plenty of choice on the menu, including vegetarian and gluten-free options.

③ ZEPHYR CAFE

38084 Cleveland Avenue, Squamish; 604-567-4568, www.zephyrcafe.ca; daily B, L and early D; $$.

This bustling café serves up nutritious fare (organic brown rice bowls, home-made veggie burgers and smoothies) that will put you in good stead for a hike or climb. There's a roaring fire when it's cold outside and sofas to get cosy.

④ RIMROCK CAFÉ & OYSTER BAR

2117 Whistler Road; tel: 604-932-5565; daily D; $$$$

Off Highway 99, 3.5km (2 miles) south of the main Whistler Village entrance, this restaurant uses top-quality local ingredients to whizz up the tempting dishes on its menu, such as venison steak with spaetzle and porcini cream sauce; wild BC salmon with fresh herbs, mashed potato and lemon beurre blanc; or confit of duck with a bacon onion dumpling and cranberry orange chutney.

⑤ THUNDERBIRD CAFÉ

Squamish Lil'Wat Cultural Centre, Whistler; tel: 604-964-0990; https://slcc.ca; Tues–Sun L; $$

Delicious meals are served here, all made with flavoursome local ingredients. Highlights include the cedar plank salmon, venison chili, and bison pot pie. There's also a choice of sandwiches, desserts such as berry crumble and lemon or date squares, and drinks including fair trade coffee and organic teas.

THE OKANAGAN

Highway 97 travels through the arid Okanagan: an enclave of orchards, vineyards, and resort towns, whose lakes, sandy beaches and scorching summers draw hordes of holiday-makers from all over the world.

DISTANCE: 176km (109 miles)
TIME: Two days
START: Osoyoos
END: Vernon
POINTS TO NOTE: Kelowna is the biggest and probably best base at any time of the year, but smaller Penticton arguably has the edge in summer when it has much more of a relaxed beach-resort vibe. Off-season you can expect room rates to halve. Scores of wineries offer tastings and wine sales – the best option is to take a wine tour and let someone else worry about driving. The wineries join together in early May and early October for annual spring and autumn wine festivals (www.thewinefestivals.com) when free wine tastings, gourmet dinners, grape stomps and vineyard picnics lure the connoisseur and novice alike.

The vine- and orchard-covered hills and warm-water lakes of the Okanagan, located in south-central BC, are about four or five hours east of Vancouver by car. Here, the geography begins to change. Rainfall is less frequent; there are arid hills. This is Canada's best-known fruit belt – the Okanagan Valley. Water from Okanagan Lake combined with hot sunny days, creates a lush garden of apples, peaches, plums, grapes, cherries, apricots, and pears.

OSOYOOS

Surrounded by scrub-covered hills, **Osoyoos** ❶ (which comes from the Syilx'tsn word *suius* for "narrowing of the waters") has one of Canada's most curious landscapes. With a mere 25cm (10in) of rain per year, this is a bona fide desert. Temperatures are regularly 10°C higher than in Nelson, less than a morning's drive away, which means exotic fruit like bananas and pomegranates can be grown. Its other great feature is Lake Osoyoos, Canada's warmest freshwater lake, with an average summer temperature of 24°C. In summer it comes alive with swimmers and boaters while streams of RVs slow-tail their way northwards.

Looking down at Osoyoos Lake

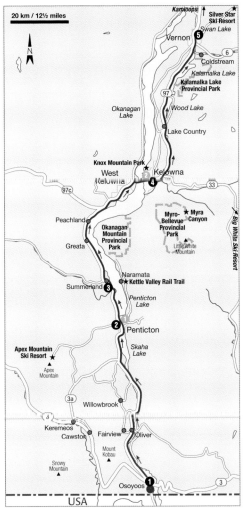

NK'MIP DESERT CULTURE CENTRE

The Osoyoos Indian Band's Nk'Mip (pronounced in-ka-meep) Desert Culture Centre (1000 Rancher Creek Road; Mar & Apr Tue–Sat 9.30am–4pm; May–mid-June daily 9.30am–4.30pm; mid-June–Aug daily 9.30am–8pm; tel: 250-495-7901; www.nkmipdesert.com) offers a well-run program of cultural events including two multi-sensory theatres showing short films, guided desert walks, and craft workshops. It's next door to Spirit Ridge and the Nk'Mip winery, Canada's first Indigenous-owned winery.

PENTICTON

Drive north on the Okanagan Highway for around 62km (38.5 miles) to **Penticton ❷**, a corruption of the Salish phrase *pen tak tin* – "a place to stay forever" and a laidback option compared to the buzz of Kelowna. Its summer daily average of 10

Okanagan beach

hours of sunshine ranks it higher than Honolulu, making tourism its biggest industry after fruit (this is "Peach City"). The town and beaches are thronged with cyclists and hikers exploring the Kettle Valley Railway (see page 64) and plenty of food and wine fans.

Spend some time in Penticton's downtown – focused on Main Street, south of Lake Okanagan – with its quirky stores and thriving bar scene. Walk north toward the lake for Penticton Art Gallery (199 Marina Way; www.pentictonartgallery.com), and make time for the lovely Penticton-Ikeda Japanese gardens behind it in the town's tiny bohemian quarter with cheap eateries and independent cafés. Try **Tacos del Norte**, see ➊, for a quick bite.

BEACHES AND SKAHA BLUFFS

Okanagan Beach is the closest sand to downtown and usually busy. At Coyote Cruises (www.coyotecruises.com), you can rent inflatable tubes for a couple of relaxing hours floating 4km (2.5 miles) south down the Okanagan River Channel to Skaha Lake, and the slightly quieter Skaha Beach.

SUMMERLAND

The agricultural community of **Summerland** ➌ is tucked away above the west side of Okanagan Lake, with an extinct volcano, Giant's Head Mountain, dominating the skyline. Summerland makes

for a pedestrian-friendly stopover to explore coffee shops along its curious mock-Tudor-style Main Street. Wine fans could do worse that pick up a bottle or two along the popular Bottleneck Drive (www.bottleneckdrive.com), which showcases 14 of the area's wineries.

KELOWNA

Kelowna ➍ ("grizzly bear" in Salish) is home to wonderful restaurants and the province's oldest vineyards; there are five wine trails in the area (see page 63). If wine's not your thing, check out microbreweries such as Tree Brewing, or Okanagan Spirits distillery, offering tours and tastings. The town has a growing arts scene, and is justifiably proud of its six-block cultural district, centred on Cawston Avenue and Water Street. Stop by the Rotary Centre for the Arts (421 Cawston Avenue; www.rotarycentreforthearts.com) and the small but impressive Kelowna Art Gallery (1315 Water Street; www.kelownaartgallery.com). The district is a great place to stay (see page 106), and for dinner there's the wonderful **Salt & Brick**, see ➋.

BEACHES

The downtown beaches off City Park and along Lakeshore Road to the south tend to attract a younger, trendier crowd: Rotary Beach here is a windsurfers' hangout, and Gyro Park, just north, is where the town's teenagers

Big White Resort   *Kelowna at dusk*

meet. Drive across the bridge to Bear Creek and Fintry provincial parks – both are lovely spots with great beaches and campgrounds.

KNOX MOUNTAIN

Getting away from Kelowna's crowds isn't easy, but you can almost shake them off by climbing Knox Mountain, the high knoll overlooking the city to the north, just five minutes' drive (or a 30min walk) from downtown. It offers lovely views over the lake and town, particularly at sunset, and there's a wooden observation tower to make the most of the panorama.

BIG WHITE SKI RESORT

Come winter, Kelowna's recreation focal point moves 56km (34.7 miles) southeast via Highway 33 to Big White Ski Resort (5315 Big White Road; Dec to mid-April; tel 250-765-3101; www.bigwhite.com). Its dry winters make this something of a powder paradise and since Big White is fairly remote, you might choose to stay in its fairly extensive resort village (though there is a Kelowna shuttle in ski season).

VERNON

Continue to the northern edge of Okanagan Lake and stop at Kalamalka Provincial Park, which sits on the stunning blue-green eponymous lake 8km (5 miles) south of **Vernon ❺**. The most popular strip of sand here is the tree-fringed Kal Beach, with convenient parking just across the railway.

Vernon itself is less frenetic than elsewhere in the region. It's a hub for golfers, with five courses in the area. You'll also find one of the country's swankiest spas here, the Swarovski crystal-studded Sparkling Hill (888 Sparkling Place; www.sparklinghill.com).

SILVER STAR MOUNTAIN RESORT

Year-round outdoor recreation is on hand at Silver Star Mountain Resort (Silver

Kelowna's vineyards

Kelowna is surrounded by some thirty wineries – many international award-winners. At one time, wines in the area focused on crisp, fruity whites and dessert wines, but now successful reds and cold-climate whites are common. It's worth visiting a couple of vineyards, since the valley's microclimates and differing soil types allow neighbouring vintners to produce completely different wines.

If you strike out on your own, try Cedar Creek Estate Winery (www.cedarcreek.bc.ca), twice voted Canada's Winery of the Year; Mission Hill Family Estate (www.missionhillwinery.com), which wouldn't look out of place in Tuscany; and Summerhill Pyramid Winery (www.summerhill.bc.ca), where wines are aged in a replica Egyptian pyramid.

Cyclist on the Kettle Valley Railway trail

Star Road, 22km east of Vernon via 48th Avenue; Nov–April; www.skisilverstar.com). The ski area has a 760m (2,493ft) vertical drop and 115 trails served by twelve lifts. In summer, a ski lift trundles to the top of Silver Star Mountain for lovely views and meadow-walking.

VERNON TO KAMLOOPS

Passing through landscapes of Eden-like clarity and beauty, Highway 97 is the best northern exit from (or entrance to, if you drive this route north to south) the Okanagan. The grass-green meadows and grazing cattle are the sort of scenery pioneers must have dreamed of and the little hamlets en route make charming spots to stay.

Kettle Valley Rail Trail

To get to the eastern trailhead from central Kelowna, drive 25km (15.5 miles) southeast on Gordon Drive, KLO Road & McCulloch Road. The Kettle Valley Railway operated from 1915 until the early 1960s until it was finally abandoned in 1989, apart from a 10-mile section, which is still used by a working steam engine. Since then great chunks of it have been part of a rails-to-trails programme (www.bcrailtrails.com) which allows you to hike or cycle for hundreds of kilometres through the region, though the key stretch is the 215km (133.5-mile) section between Midway and Penticton. Its greatest spectacle is Myra Canyon above Kelowna, where the series of gigantic wooden trestles provide an impressive testament to engineering. From the eastern trailhead you can walk or cycle out and back along the trestles for an hour or two, or even cycle all the way to Penticton, an eight-to nine-hour ride with gorgeous scenery below. You'll need someone to pick you up at the other end; Monashee Adventure Tours in Kelowna (www.monashee adventuretours.com) offers this service, along with bike rentals.

Food and Drink

① TACOS DEL NORTE

86 Backstreet blvd, Penticton; tel: 250 689 2453, www.tacosdelnorte.ca; daily L & early D; $
Delicious made-from-scratch authentic Baja-style tacos with local ingredients including organic cheese, house-made sauces and salsas. All of the food is exceedingly fresh and and the service is fantastic; a perfect spot to laze on the patio with a locally brewed beer.

② SALT & BRICK

243 Bernard Avenue, Kelowna; tel: 250 484 3234, www.saltandbrick.ca; daily D; $$
Excellent casual spot serving shared plates of house-cured meats and artisan cheeses alongside wines from the Pacific Northwest. Seating in wooden booths or stools at the bar.

Revelstoke Ski Resort

REVELSTOKE TO THE ROCKIES

*To drive the Trans-Canada (Highway 1) from Revelstoke –
Canada's backcountry-ski capital – toward the Rockies is to find
that its jaw-clanging, breath-taking, beautiful mountain scenery.*

DISTANCE: 226km (140 miles)
TIME: Two days
START: Revelstoke
END: Lake O'Hara, Yoho National Park
POINTS TO NOTE: A vast proportion of parkland is wilderness and there are no services on the Trans-Canada between Revelstoke and Golden. Park Canada experts monitor the slopes, and at dangerous times they close the Highway and call in the Canadian Armed Forces, who bring down avalanches before they become a threat. There is single park entry fee, which includes all the National Parks along this route. The parks have superb campsites; for provincial parks camping and backcountry camping, passes must be purchased separately. Golden is the nearest town to Glacier and Yoho National Parks and here, or Field, is a good place to stay overnight (see page 106). Take advantage of the hiking and biking trails; other activities – fishing, skiing, canoeing, cycling, rock climbing and so on – are comprehensively dealt with in the visitor centres.

REVELSTOKE

Revelstoke ❶ is divided between a motel-and-garage strip along the highway and a dispersed collection of houses downtown. If you want to relax, try warm-watered Williamson Lake, a favourite swimming spot for locals which also has a pleasant campground (see page 107). Downtown, the small but polished Revelstoke Railway Museum (719 Track Street West; www.railwaymuseum.com) has memorabilia relating to the building of the Canadian Pacific Railway, and a few blocks away farm-to-table **Terra Firma Kitchen**, see ❶.

REVELSTOKE MOUNTAIN RESORT

Revelstoke Mountain Resort (2950 Camozzi Road, 6km (3.7 miles) south east of town; Dec to mid-April; tel 250-814-0087; www.revelstokemountain resort.com) has a solid national reputation as a superb skiing spot thanks to its rugged terrain and huge 1713m (5,620ft) vertical drop – North America's highest. About half of the hill is geared to

The view from Mount Revelstoke across the forest

experts, and only a couple of the 52 runs are beginner-level.

MOUNT REVELSTOKE NATIONAL PARK

The smallest national park in the region, **Mount Revelstoke National Park** ❷ was created in 1914 to protect the Clachnacudainn Range of the Columbia Mountains. The Trans-Canada Highway runs just inside the park's boundary for 13km (8 miles) along its southern

perimeter and boasts views of forests and snow-capped peaks aplenty.

THE MEADOWS-IN-THE-SKY-PARKWAY

The main access point to the park interior is the easily accessed **Meadows-in-the-Sky-Pass** ❸. It opens when the road is snow-free, usually from May to early October. Strike north from the Trans-Canada Highway at Revelstoke and wind up the switchbacks through forest and

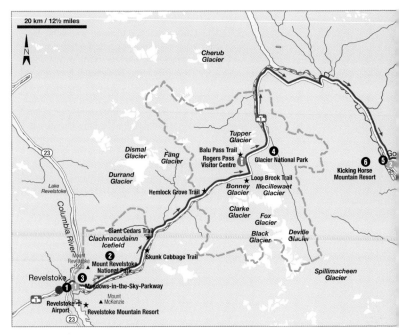

Skiers hiking in Glacier National Park

alpine meadows with glorious displays of wildflowers. A gate lies 1km (0.6 miles) shy of the summit at Balsam Lake where you can take a regular shuttle bus (daily 10am–4.30pm) to the summit.

GLACIER NATIONAL PARK

Glacier National Park ❹ protects the Selkirk Mountains in the Columbia Mountain Range. Canada's second oldest national park, these glacier-clad mountains are credited with being the birthplace of sport mountaineering in Canada. Here weather systems from the Pacific meet the mountains making for highly variable conditions – you can set off in blazing sunshine and meet a blizzard by lunchtime – but despite this, the soaring alpine scenery and vast wilderness attracts climbers, backcountry skiers and hikers from across the world.

GOLDEN

Once you leave the eastern perimeter of Glacier National Park, it's 60km (37 miles) before you reach **Golden ❺**, the midway point between the Columbia and Rocky Mountains, and the nearest town to Glacier and Yoho national parks. The modest little town straddles the Columbia River, below the highway;

Heli- and catskiing

The only way to get up into the deep powder is via snowcat or helicopter, but neither are especially cheap; expect to pay around $550 for a day cat skiing and $1000 for heli-skiing. Day packages are available but multiday lodge-based options are best if you want to explore untouched terrain and experience backcountry skiing at its best.

Contact K-3 Cat Skiing (tel: 250-837-5100, www.k3catski.com); Revelstoke Mountain Resort (see page 65) or Selkirk Wilderness Skiing (tel: 250-366-4424, www.selkirkwilderness.com).

explore and you'll find an up-and-coming place that's beginning to make its mark as a ski town and mountain-biking destination. Try **Bacchus Books & Café**, see , for coffee on the riverfront patio.

KICKING HORSE MOUNTAIN RESORT

Step out of the Golden Eagle Gondola, the main lift at **Kicking Horse Mountain Resort** ❻ (1500 Kicking Horse Trail, 13km from Golden; tel 888-706-1117, www.kickinghorseresort.com), at the top of its ascent, and into a wonderland of clouds and peaks.

From June to September its gondola is also well worth riding for the views, along with the option of eating at **Eagles Eye**, see ❸. There's also a world-class mountain-biking park and a grizzly bear refuge.

YOHO NATIONAL PARK

Yoho National Park's ❼ name derives from a Cree word meaning "wonder" – testament to the grandeur of its mountains, lakes and waterfalls.

The only settlement, Field, has the park visitor centre and limited accommodation. More accommodation is available at trail hubs – Lake O'Hara, the Yoho Valley and Emerald Lake – the start of stunning hiking routes and the main focal points of the park. If you have time for just a single day-walk, make it the Iceline–Whaleback–Twin Falls Trail. If you're really short on time, get a quick taste of the park on the side roads to Emerald Lake and the Yoho Valley.

EMERALD LAKE AND THE YOHO VALLEY

Emerald Lake ❽ and the adjacent **Yoho Valley** ❾ spread north of the Trans-Canada and are relatively accessible for a casual visit. The Emerald Lake Road leaves the highway west of Field and

---

Field's railway

Regular passenger services no longer come through Field, but the railway is among among the first things you see. The railway was as much a political as a transportation tool, designed to unite the country and encourage settlement. A northerly route would have ignored great tracts of valuable prairie near the US border (around Calgary), and allowed much of the area and its resources to slip into the hands of the US. So, against all engineering advice, the railway was cajoled into taking the Kicking Horse route, and thus obliged to negotiate four-percent grades, the greatest of any commercial railway of the time. The result was the famed Spiral Tunnels, two vast figure-of-eight galleries within the mountains; from a viewpoint east of Field on Highway 1, you can watch goods trains emerge from the tunnels before the rear wagons have even entered.

Kayaking on Emerald Lake in Yoho National Park

ends at Emerald Lake Lodge. Alternatively, the Yoho Valley Road leaves the Trans-Canada east of Field and is a narrow, summer-only affair that's unsuitable for trailers and RVs. Though these areas lack the magic of O'Hara, they still offer amazing sights – such as Takakkaw Falls – great trails and mesmerizing scenery.

FIELD

No more than a few wooden houses backed by an amphitheatre of sheer-drop mountains, **Field** ⑩ looks like an old-world pioneer settlement, little changed from its 1884 origins as a railroad-construction camp. Field has a few interesting attractions nearby – the Burgess Shale, a unique geological formation on the upper slopes of Mount Field with the fossils from the Middle Cambrian period (515–530 million years ago), and the Spiral Tunnels (see page 68) – but it's mostly a base for hikers. It does have one very good restaurant (see page 115).

LAKE O'HARA

The **Lake O'Hara** ⑪ area, in the southeastern corner of the park, is one of the Rockies' finest all-round enclaves – with staggering scenery, numerous lakes and an immense diversity of alpine and subalpine terrain. It's a great base for hiking: you could easily spend a fortnight exploring the trails that strike out from the central lodge and campground. The setting is matchless, with Lake O'Hara framed

by two of the peaks that also overlook Lake Louise across the ridge – mounts Lefroy (3429m) and Victoria (3464m).

Food and drink

① TERRA FIRMA KITCHEN

415 A Victoria Road, Revelstoke; tel: 250-805-0646, http://terrafirmakitchen.ca; daily B & L; $$

A farm-to-table restaurant whose extensive breakfast menu (from 6am) includes bacon and egg sandwiches with tomato jam on sourdough, and lunch has daily changing salads, frittatas, and mouth-watering toasties slathered with brown butter.

② BACCHUS BOOKS & CAFÉ

409 9th Avenue N, Golden; tel: 250-344-5600, www.bacchusbooks.ca; daily B & L; $

Relaxed café where you can combine browsing thousands of books with a coffee in the upstairs café or on the pretty riverfront patio. The food is also delicious.

③ EAGLES EYE

Kicking Horse Mountain Resort, 13km from Golden; tel: 250-439-5425, www.kickinghorseresort.com; Mon–Thu & Sun L; Fri & Sat L & D; $$$

The highest restaurant in the country has the kind of views you'd expect, and food is a cut above the usual tourist fare. At lunchtime, appetizers and entrees might include fried calamari and a steak sandwich; weekend dinners are a little swankier.

VICTORIA: DOWNTOWN AND AROUND

Victoria is considerably smaller than Vancouver, a comfortable and easy-going place of small-town values, a pretty waterfront, excellent restaurants, the superb Royal British Columbia Museum, and a decidedly English ambience.

DISTANCE: 4.5km (2.8 miles)
TIME: 5 hours (not including wandering around Beacon Hill Park)
START: Visitor Centre, 812 Wharf Street
END: Beacon Hill Park
POINTS TO NOTE: With two cathedrals on this route, Sunday is probably not the best day to choose unless you want to attend a service. Otherwise, check on their websites to ascertain the most suitable times to look around and the possibility of a choir practice or organ recital. If you're here between early September and May, the Maritime Museum will be closed on Monday and tours will only be available on Saturday at 1pm. To visit the Legislative Assembly you'll need to go through security and have some form of valid photo ID (a passport is ideal). Self-guided visits are only available on weekdays during the summer season (mid–May to early Sep), otherwise you have to join one of the regular guided tours, but reservations are not necessary.

On this route, you'll visit the maritime museum, two impressive cathedral buildings, and the characterful streets in the heart of the city's most interesting shopping district. The route then heads back toward the Inner Harbour and beyond to take in some fine art, the grandiose, domed Legislative Assembly building, the splendid provincial museum, and Beacon Hill Park.

MARITIME MUSEUM OF BRITISH COLUMBIA

Starting from the Tourist Information Center at the corner of Government and Wharf streets, cross at the lights as if you were walking up Government Street, then swivel right and cross to Humboldt Street. Go along Humboldt to the end where you'll find the **Maritime Museum of British Columbia** ❶ (634 Humboldt Street; tel: 250-385-4222; www.mmbc.bc.ca; daily 10am–5pm, closed Mon early Sep–mid-May). Maritime exploration and trade hold a particularly important place in the city's history, and this fine museum has a superb collection, amounting to around

A view of the Inner Harbour with the Legislative Assembly building lit up

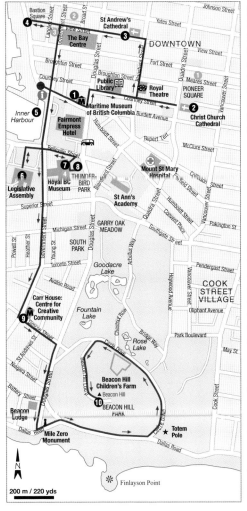

35,000 objects dating back to 1775 and huge collections of maps, photographs, ships' plans, and more. Added to this are three historic vessels, the Dorothy, the Tilikum, and the Trekka, the smallest craft ever to sail around the globe.

CHRIST CHURCH CATHEDRAL

From the Maritime Museum, go left along Douglas Street for one block, turning right onto Courtney Street. Continue forward, cross Blanchard Street and then Quadra Street via the pedestrian crossing to reach **Christ Church Cathedral** ❷ (tel: 250-383-2714; www. christchurchcathedral. bc.ca).

In cathedral terms, this one is relatively young. The initial part was consecrated in 1929 and the most recent addition was finished in the 1990s, but the design is Gothic, giving it a grandeur befitting its status as the episcopal seat of the Bishop of the Diocese of British

Inside St Andrew's Cathedral

Columbia. Inside, there are no less than three organs, several features from religious buildings in England, and some fine stained glass. The cathedral hosts performances of classical, chamber, choral, and organ music.

If you're ready for a snack or a drink, the **Blue Fox Café**, see ❶, is close by – go north on Quadra Street past Pioneer Square and take the second right onto Fort Street.

ST ANDREW'S CATHEDRAL

Exiting from the front entrance of Christ Church Cathedral, retrace your steps down Courtney Street to Blanchard Street and then take a right. Cross Broughton Street and continue along Blanchard, which is lined with shops and restaurants, then cross Fort Street and at the next intersection (View Street) stands **St Andrew's Cathedral** ❸ (740 View Street; tel: 250-388-5571; http://standrews cathedral.com). This is Victoria's Roman Catholic cathedral, a beautiful High Victorian building, tastefully elaborate both outside and in, with an elegant, soaring tower 53 metres (175ft) tall. Dating from 1892, its notable features include the splendid altar and carved lectern, both built by Indigenous artists – Charles Elliot and Roy Henry Vickers respectively.

BASTION SQUARE

From the front door of St Andrew's, turn right then immediately right again to walk along the side of the cathedral, heading down View Street, with the CIBC building visible ahead on the right. Continue past CIBC and cross Douglas Street, keeping straight ahead between the Bay Centre and McDonald's. Continue down View Street until you reach Government Street. Here, an archway heralds the entrance to **Bastion Square** ❹. The square is actually a narrow pedestrian-only street lined by vendors selling all kinds of art and crafts, trinkets, and plants. It makes for an engaging stroll back down to Wharf Street and the harbour.

Butchart Gardens

If you're into things horticultural, trek out to the celebrated Butchart Gardens, 23km (14 miles) north of Victoria, on a sheltered peninsula on the Saanich Inlet. The gardens were started in 1904 by Jennie Butchart, wife of a mine-owner and pioneer of Portland Cement in Canada and the US, her initial aim being to landscape one of her husband's quarries. The garden now comprises Japanese and Italian gardens and numerous decorative cameos. About half a million visitors a year wander through the foliage, which includes over a million plants and seven hundred different species. The gardens are renowned for the firework displays that usually take place each Saturday evening from late June to early September, and are often followed by open-air concerts. See www.butchart-gardens.com.

Busy Bastion Square

From here, there are plenty more shopping streets to explore, and, off Government Street (left after exiting back through the Bastion Square Arch, then a little way along on the right) tiny Trounce Alley has some high-end boutiques, art galleries and places for refreshment, including **The Tapa Bar**, see ❷. **The Churchill**, see ❸, is another good option – and even better if you come back after dark for drinks at the bar.

If you're happy to add another short stretch to the walk, continue along Government street as far as Fisguard Street, turn right to reach Douglas Street, then left on Douglas. The Victoria Public Market at the Hudson, where you'll find local produce, is in a big white building on the right.

INNER HARBOUR

Walk south on Government Street, past your starting point toward the **Inner Harbour ❺**, the heart and soul of Victoria. Pleasure boats bob on the water, seaplanes take off, buskers entertain, and people hang out to enjoy the scene. Completing the set-piece are the grand and imposing buildings of the Fairmont Empress Hotel at the head of the harbour and the Legislative Assembly building on the southern side. The Fairmont Empress Hotel is a National Historic Site of Canada, and it's worth making a reservation for one of their traditional (pricey) English-style afternoon teas, or go in to take a look at the magnificent lobby.

LEGISLATIVE ASSEMBLY

The **Legislative Assembly ❻** (tel: 250-387-3046; www.leg.bc.ca; Mon–Fri 9am–5pm mid-May–early Sep, daily 8.30am–4.30pm early Sep–mid May) is an imposing building, built using mostly local materials and completed between

Southern Gulf Islands

Scattered between Vancouver Island and the mainland lie several hundred tiny islands, most no more than lumps of rock, a few large enough to hold permanent populations and warrant a regular ferry service. Two main clusters are accessible from Victoria: the Southern Gulf Islands and the San Juan Islands, both part of the same archipelago, except that the San Juan group is in the United States.

You get a good look at the Southern Gulf Islands on the seaplanes from Vancouver or on the ferry from Tsawwassen, the coastline makes for superb sailing, and an armada of small boats criss-crosses between the islands for most of the year. Hikers and campers are also well served, and fishing is good, with the surrounding waters holding some of the world's biggest salmon. There's also an abundance of marine wildlife (sea lions, orcas, seals, bald eagles, herons, cormorants). For full details of what's happening on the islands, grab a copy of the Gulf Islander, distributed at the island visitor centres and at ferry terminals.

The legislative Assembly building

1897 and 1915. On the lawns in front is a statue of Queen Victoria, who gave her name to the city. The figure up on top of the dome is of Captain George Vancouver (see page 11).

The interior of the building is equally grand, with stained-glass windows, gilding, murals, and other artwork, and the tour takes in a number of sumptuously decorated rooms. The experience is enhanced in summer and occasional off-season days by the Parliamentary Players, a theatrical group of students who bring to life notable figures from BC history. It's also possible to watch the government in action. Come back after dark to see the entire building lit up.

ROYAL BC MUSEUM AND THUNDERBIRD PARK

Cross Government Street to the Royal BC Museum. One of the finest museums in Canada, the **Royal BC Museum ❼** (675 Belleville Street; tel: 250-356-7226; www.royalbcmuseum.bc.ca; Mon, Tue & Thu–Sun 10am–6pm) was established in 1886, and grew in content and stature to necessitate new premises, which were built in the 1960s and 70s. Highlights of the collection include a wonderful array of Indigenous art and other displays detailing some 10,000 years of their history and culture. Other human history is covered, along with art collections, natural history exhibits, and much more. There are regular themed exhibitions, and the museum has an IMAX theater.

Behind the museum, at the southwest corner of Belleville and Douglas streets, is little **Thunderbird Park ❽**, established to house a number of the museum's totem poles. These were later moved into the museum building to protect them from deterioration, and replicas were created for the park and further poles added by the Kwakwaka'wakw master carver, Chief Mungo Martin. He also built the traditional-style Mungo Martin House in the park, now owned by his grandson and used for First Nations events. Its structure and contents give a splendid overview of the culture and heritage of the Kwakwaka'wakw people. Before moving on, grab a coffee and a baked treat in the museum's **Sequoia Coastal Coffee**, see ❹, or check out the food trucks out in the rear courtyard.

CARR HOUSE: CENTRE FOR CREATIVE COMMUNITY

Walk south on Government Street until you reach the block between Marifield Avenue and Simcoe Street. Here you'll find the **Carr House: Centre for Creative Community ❾** (207 Government Street; tel: 250-383-5843; https://carrhouse.ca; daily 11am–4pm). A National Historic Site of Canada and Provincial Historic Site, it used to be the family home of Emily Carr (1871–1945), the renowned artist, writer, environmentalist, and social justice advocate. Restored and furnished as it would have been when she was living there, it still

Beacon Hill Park

feels like a welcoming home rather than a museum.

BEACON HILL PARK

From here, round the corner onto Simcoe Street and continue to Douglas Street. **Beacon Hill Park** ⑩ is across the road, but first turn right on Douglas Street and walk down to see the Terry Fox Statue (see page 37) and the Mile Zero Monument. Though not particularly impressive, it does have some cachet as the starting point of the 8,000km- (5,000-mile) plus Trans-Canada Highway. Continue around the circular road with the water on your right and you'll soon come to the world's tallest free-standing totem pole; carved by Mungo Martin, the 'Spirit of Lekwammen' stands at 38.9 metres (128ft).

In the park, tree-studded lawns invite wandering, as well as few playgrounds and sports facilities, including tennis courts, a baseball diamond and – a rarity in Canada – a cricket pitch (a testament to Victoria's Britishness). The Cameron Bandshell (tel: 250-361-0246 for information) has a schedule of free concerts, lunchtime shows for children, and social dances from June to September.

Food and Drink

① BLUE FOX CAFÉ

101–919 Fort Street; tel: 250-380-1683; www.thebluefoxcafe.com; Mon, Tue & Thu–Sun; B and L; $

All-day breakfasts are popular with Victoria's late risers, but the early-bird special is worth setting your alarm clock for. Snacks and lunch items feature ethically raised, free-range, and vegetarian items with some exotic influences – Moroccan chicken quesadillas, for instance.

② THE TAPA BAR

620 Trounce Alley; tel: 250-383-0013; http://tapabar.ca; daily L and D; $$

This is a trendy spot with a huge and interesting variety of tapas, including gluten free and vegan. The very good wine list includes some local wines and they have a small heated patio.

③ THE CHURCHILL

1140 Government Street; tel: 250-384-6835; http://thechurchill.ca; daily L and D; $$

A cozy but refined bar with a good-value traditional menu enlivened by some international accents such as Middle Eastern layer dip or Vietnamese lettuce wraps. Specials might include a house-made pot pie or beer-battered fish. There's a long list of craft beers and cocktails to help the food go down.

④ SEQUOIA COASTAL COFFEE

Royal BC Museum, 675 Belleville Street; tel: 778-265-9393; http://sequoiacoffee.ca; daily B and L; $

Craft coffee topped with creative swirls of cream, plus sandwiches and baked goods made to traditional local recipes, hit the spot here.

Inside the Art Gallery of Greater Victoria

VICTORIA: ROCKLAND AND GONZALES

This route explores a superb art gallery, a lavish historic mansion, and two glorious gardens, none of which will prepare you for the final destination – a wild and rocky place with a stunning view over the Juan de Fuca Strait.

DISTANCE: 3.4km (2.1 miles)

TIME: 4 hours

START: Art Gallery of Greater Victoria

END: Gonzales Park

POINTS TO NOTE: There are no restaurants or coffee shops along this route, but Craigdarroch Castle, Government House, and Abkhazi Garden all have tea rooms; check opening times if you are relying on these for refreshments. Otherwise, you should plan for a picnic. Government House is only open once a month for tours (the website will be able to provide the dates), but the beautiful gardens and Cary Castle Mews can be visited every day. Gonzales Park is steep and rocky, and be aware that it's quite a long way down to and back up from the beach. Don't miss the view from the top, though. Buses 1, 3 and 4 from downtown will get you fairly close to the Art Gallery. To get back from the end point of our route, bus 7 runs along Fairfield Road to downtown.

ART GALLERY OF GREATER VICTORIA

Opened in 1951 in a leafy suburb of the city, the **Art Gallery of Greater Victoria ❶** (1040 Moss Street; www.aggv. ca; Tue, Wed & Fri, Sat 10am–5pm, Thu 1–9pm, Sun noon–5pm) originally occupied the historic Spencer Mansion next door, but by 1955 more space was needed, and by 1978 its current seven galleries had been built. The Spencer Mansion is now the gallery shop and offices.

Among the highlights is the collection of memorabilia and paintings by the renowned local artist, Emily Carr, whose former home in Victoria is open to the public (see page 74). Her bold Post-Impressionist style is clearly influenced by her absorbing interest in First Nations art and culture, in which she immersed herself for extended periods of time, and in the nature that surrounded her on Vancouver Island. The gallery also has an excellent collection of Asian art and artifacts, including fine carvings, complemented by a delight-

Craigdarroch Castle

ful Asian garden where you'll find North America's only authentic Japanese Shinto shrine. The gallery also hosts special exhibitions and events, including workshops and Family Sundays.

CRAIGDARROCH CASTLE

From the gallery, go north on Moss Street and right on Fort Street, then take the first right on Joan Crescent, and follow the green signs. The castle will appear on the right.

A National Historic Site of Canada, **Craigdarroch Castle** ❷ (1050 Joan Crescent; www.thecastle.ca; reduced hours Fri, Sat & Sun 10.30am–4pm) is a huge Gothic mansion which was built in the late 1880s for the Scottish magnate, politician, and all-round sharp-practitioner Robert Dunsmuir for the princely sum of $200,000. Not the

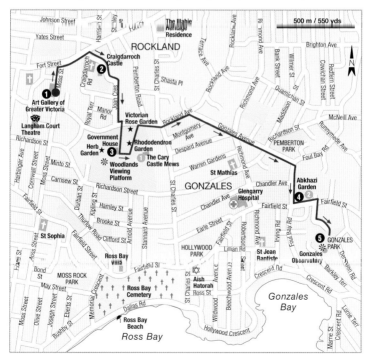

Abkhazi Garden

most considerate or safety-conscious employer, some might say he got his comeuppance by dying before his 'castle' was finished. Later it was put to better use as a war veterans' hospital and an outpost of Montréal's McGill University. Now it's in the hands of the Castle Society, a registered charity, who maintain the building and its extravagant decor. Concerts, theatrical performances, and classic movie screenings are also hosted here.

GOVERNMENT HOUSE

From Craigdarroch Castle, continue south on Joan Crescent to reach Rockland Avenue. There are three ways into the grounds, one to the right (this is the vehicle entrance) as you stand at the end of Joan Crescent and two more a little further along Rockland Avenue to the left.

The official residence of the Lieutenant Governor of British Columbia, which also accommodates visiting British royalty, **Government House** ❸ (1401 Rockland Avenue; www.ltgov.bc.ca) has beautiful grounds and gardens that the public can explore at will, including a hiking trail through the Garry Oak Woodlands behind the house. Points of non-horticultural interest around the gardens include the 7.3-metre (24ft-) Hosaqami totem pole and a bronze statue of Sir James Douglas (the 'father of British Columbia').

Carey Castle Mews, on the grounds, is where the stables and carriage house used to be, along with a gaol and various domestic buildings. It includes Butterworth Cottage and the lovely **Rudi's Tea Room**, see ❶, which is open seasonally.

ABKHAZI GARDEN

Leave the Government House grounds onto Rockland Avenue and turn right, then make a right onto Gonzales Avenue. At the end, where it meets Foul Bay Road, turn right, then later go left on Fairfield Road. The garden is on the left.

Lieutenant Governor

Under the Canadian Constitution, the head of state is the British monarch, represented in Canada by a Governor General and a Queen's Privy Council for Canada. Their duties include appointing a Lieutenant Governor for each of the Canadian provinces, to represent the monarch. The post involves officiating at ceremonial events, hosting important official visitors and various behind-the-scenes and advisory activities. British Columbia's current Lieutenant Governor, appointed in 2018, is The Honourable Janet Austin, a former CEO of the Vancouver YWCA and active volunteer for a number of charitable organizations.

Gonzales Observatory and Park overlooking the bay

Covering only 0.4 hectares (1 acre), and tucked away in a residential area, **Abkhazi Garden** ❹ (1964 Fairfield Road; www.abkhaziteahouse.com; daily 11am–5pm Apr–Sep, Wed–Sun 11am–4pm Oct–Mar) is well worth seeking out. Garden lovers will delight in the design, romantics will revel in the story of how it came to be, and everyone will enjoy the great afternoon teas served in the **Teahouse**, see ❷. The garden's story begins in 1946, when Prince and Princess Abkhazi came to live here. Finally reunited after several long years of painful and lonely separation before and during World War II, they got their fairytale ending here; they really did live happily ever after. Together they created the garden on the rocky slope and devoted their lives to each other and maintaining what they saw as a symbol of their love.

GONZALES PARK

From Abkhazi Garden it's about a six-minute walk to **Gonzales Park** ❺. Leaving the garden, go east on Fairfield Road then right onto Fairfield Place. At the Denison Road intersection, turn right.

This small park will probably come as something of a surprise amid an otherwise typical residential neighborhood. No neatly manicured lawns and flower beds here – it's a wild and rocky landscape, with a wonderful view out over the Juan de Fuca Strait, espe-cially from the landmark white building of the old Observatory at the top of the hill. You'll see a sandy beach on a semicircular bay down below, and it's accessible if you have the stamina.

When it's time to leave, retrace your steps to Fairfield Road for bus 7 back to downtown.

Food and Drink

❶ RUDI'S TEA ROOM
Government House Mews, 1401 Rockland Avenue; tel: 250-590-3953; http://ltgov.bc.ca/tea-room; mid-May–Sep, Tue–Sat L; $
House-made soup, made from Government House garden produce, sandwiches made from house-baked bread, and tasty quiches can be followed by freshly-baked scones and cakes.

❷ THE TEAHOUSE AT ABKHAZI GARDEN
Abkhazi Garden; 1964 Fairfield Road; tel: 778-265-6466; www.abkhaziteahouse.com; Wed–Sat L; $ except for Royal High Tea $$$
There's a real English feel to the elevenses, the afternoon tea, and the sumptuous four-course Royal Abkhazi High Tea. Each offers various quantities of sandwiches, house-baked scones, and cakes. The short lunch menu offers soup, salad, crêpes, and a charcuterie board, and there's a tempting dessert menu.

Thetis Lake Regional Park

COWICHAN VALLEY AND NANAIMO

This route heads out to explore some artsy small towns, as well as Vancouver Island's second city, Nanaimo, rich in Indigenous culture and glorious scenery; visit some Cowichan Valley wineries for good measure.

DISTANCE: 113km (70 miles)
TIME: 3 days
START: Victoria
END: Nanaimo
POINTS TO NOTE: If you're planning to visit any Cowichan Valley vineyards, check their websites first as some are only open seasonally, and may not be open every day, but may accept visitors by appointment. Some offer free tastings, while others will charge, but they may take the price off any purchases you make. It's easy to underestimate how many small sips you might have on a tour of several vineyards, so have a designated driver or find an organized tour providing transportation.

It only takes around two hours to drive up the TransCanada Highway from Victoria to Nanaimo, but there is so much to see and do along the way that it can easily occupy days of exploring.

The early part of the route skirts the Thetis Lake Regional Park and runs right through the Goldstream Provincial Park.

Later it climbs above the Saanich Inlet, and there are a couple of places where you can pull off the highway to enjoy the amazing views. At intervals along the highway, blue road signs point you in the direction of various tourist attractions, so turn off to any that take your fancy. There are also small Wine Route signs, indicating turn-offs to nearby vineyards. All are worth a detour if they are open.

MALAHAT SKYWALK

The best stop to take in the Saanich Peninsula view is around 30 minutes north of Victoria. The **Malahat SkyWalk** ❶ (www.malhayskywalk.com) has a viewing platform at the top of a wooden spiral tower. There's an emphasis on nature and your visit includes an elevated treetop walk.

DUNCAN, CITY OF TOTEMS

If you're ready for lunch, park in downtown **Duncan** ❷ and head for **Café la Vie**, see ❶, before setting out to explore this pleasant town. It boasts a collection of 40 colourful totem poles dotted around

Totem poles in Duncan

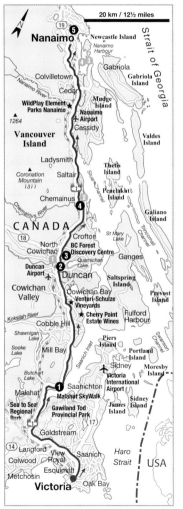

the downtown streets to celebrate the fact that the town lies on the traditional lands of the Quw'utsun' (Cowichan) people. Yellow footprints painted onto the sidewalks mark the route of the Totems Tour Walk, or you can take a free one-hour guided tour (Mon–Fri, on the hour, 10am–2pm mid-June–mid-Sep; rest of year by appointment for a small fee), departing from the train station at 130 Canada Avenue.

The historic core of the town also contains an interesting range of shops, including art and craft galleries selling the work of local artists and artisans. City Square is the focal point for events and hosts the Saturday farmers' market.

Stay overnight in Duncan (see page 107) and check what's on. The Cowichan Performing Arts Centre (cowichanpac.ca) stages a full program of theater, dance, concerts, and movies. The Duncan Showroom (www.showroomproductions. ca) is a live music venue and, if it's high season there should be something going on in Charles Hoey Park or City Square.

COWICHAN VALLEY MUSEUM

The Cowichan Valley Museum & Archives (130 Canada Avenue; www.cowichan valleymuseum.bc.ca; reduced hours Thu 11am–3pm) is housed in the heritage train station, hence the big red CN locomotive parked outside. There are a number of totem poles around the building. Inside the museum is a re-created general store, exhibits on life in the valley, and a collection of historic medical equipment.

One of Chemainus' many murals

BC FOREST DISCOVERY CENTRE

Next morning, a very short distance north from Duncan, you can stop at the **BC Forest Discovery Centre** ❸ (http://bcforestdiscoverycentre.com; daily 10am–4.30pm June–early Sept, Thu–Mon 10am–4.30pm May and rest of Sept; open for special events only the rest of the year). This is a great place to find out more about all those trees you've been driving past. The sprawling site includes a replica logging camp and various equipment and vehicles, forest trails, and a lookout tower with a great view. The highlight of the visit, though, is the 2.5-km (1.6-mile) ride on a narrow-gauge train pulled by one of the museum's heritage locomotives, which takes you through the forest and over the water via the Somenos Lake trestle.

CHEMAINUS

Some blue signs for artisans and a couple of billboards announce the approach to the turnoff for **Chemainus** ❹. At the lights, turn right onto Henry Road and at the traffic circle go left onto Chemainus Road for downtown.

The town is best known for the giant murals that adorn various buildings – 45 at the time of writing. Yellow footprints on sidewalks show the mural route, plus there are sculptures dotted around town, too. The Chemainus Valley Museum (9799 Water Wheel Crescent; www.chemainusvalleymuseum.ca; daily 11am–3pm Feb–mid-Dec) is in the center of town in Water Wheel Park, with a good viewpoint nearby.

This little town is also home to many local artisan studios and craft shops that invite browsing, as well as some good cafés and restaurants, including the **Owl's Nest Bakery and Bistro**, see ❷. The highly-regarded Chemainus Theatre Festival stages around eight major productions during the year, and St Michael's Church on Mill Street hosts classical music concerts.

> ## The Warm Land
>
> The Quw'utsun people, the valley's original inhabitants, referred to Cowichan as 'the warm land', and it does indeed have something of a European climate, albeit more akin to the Mosel region than Bordeaux. Initially, planting vines here was an experiment, but now there are enough wineries to warrant a Wine Trail (www.cheerscowichan.com; vancouverislandwinetours.com). Visit in late August and you can attend the two-day Cowichan Wine Festival (www.tourismcowichan.com/wine-festival), with live music and foodie events. In addition to the dozen or so wineries in the Cowichan region, there are also craft breweries and distilleries, a cider-maker, and Canada's only tea farm, the Westholme Tea Company. Full details are available at www.tourismcowichan.com/activities/sip-savour.

Fishing boats in Nanaimo harbour

When you've done all you want to do in Chemainus, get back onto the Trans-Canada highway and press on north to spend the night in accommodation in Nanaimo (see page 108).

NANAIMO

Nanaimo ❺ is famous – in Canada at least – for the Nanaimo Bar, a three-layer confection of custard and chocolate ganache on top of a coconut and crumb base, but it has much more to offer than a few inches on the waistline. Long the home of the Snunéymuxw people, one of the Coast Salish cultures, Nanaimo is Vancouver Island's second-largest city, with a large and attractive harbour, a strong First Nations culture, a creative community of artists, artisans, writers, and musicians, and a backdrop of forested mountains. There's plenty going on here, the shopping opportunities are exceptionally good, and there are fantastic places to eat and drink. Downtown, the narrow old streets make for pleasant wandering, lined by colourful stores, including a large number of independent retailers and quality art and craft galleries. Eat breakfast or lunch at **Gabriel's Gourmet Café**, see ❸.

HARBOURFRONT WALKWAY

A morning walk along the Harbourfront Walkway makes for a great introduction to the city. Start at the Front Street end, opposite the Port Theatre. Along the way you'll see seaplanes taking off or landing, the Fisherman's Market, and boats galore, including fishing charters, whale-watching trips, and ferries to off-shore islands and to Horseshoe Bay on the BC mainland.

Take time to take in the views, and, in the early stages at least, there's no shortage of places to get refreshment. Try the **Javawocky Coffee House**, see ❹. Behind here, and you may have spotted the flag flying from its pointed roof, is the white-painted Bastion (98 Front Street; http://nanaimomuseum.ca; daily 10am–4pm, reduced hours off season), a three-storey historic relic of the Hudson's Bay Company dating from 1853. Continuing along the walkway, it soon gets less commercialized. From Maffeo Sutton Park, a ferry leaves to the Newcastle Island Provincial Marine Park, visible offshore. The island, *Sysutshun* in the Snuneymuxw language, is a rewarding place to explore, which can be greatly enhanced with a Snuneymuxs First Nation guide.

As you continue along the walkway, you'll eventually pass the marina of the Nanaimo Yacht Club, with residential buildings closing in on the left before the walk comes to an end at an industrial area. You can walk back downtown on the Trans-Canada Highway, but it's not much of an inspiring walk with little to see. Better, really, to turn around and retrace your steps back along the water to take in the views a second time.

A seaplane taking off from Nanaimo harbour

NANAIMO MUSEUM AND ART GALLERY

It was a Snunéymuxw chief who first spoke of coal in the area, which turned out to be one of the largest deposits of the 'black gold' on the North American west coast. There's an excellent exhibit about this, including a representation of a mine shaft, in the Nanaimo Museum (100 Museum Way; http://nanaimomuseum.ca; daily 10am–4pm mid-May–early Sep, Mon–Sat 10am–4pm early Sep–mid-May), which also delves back into the history of the First Nations.

The Nanaimo Art Gallery (150 Commercial Street; http://nanaimogallery.ca; Tue–Sat 10am–5pm, Sun noon–5pm) has a fine collection, and the Arts Labs provide for some hands-on creativity for all ages.

At the end of the day in Nanaimo, it's a straight drive back down the Trans-Canada Highway to Victoria – or choose to stay another night here and then explore more Cowichan Valley Wineries, perhaps with a side trip to lovely Lake Cowichan on your way south.

Food and Drink

1 CAFÉ LA VIE
171 Canada Avenue, Duncan; tel: 250-597-8168; www.facebook.com/duncancafelavie; daily B and L; $
Whether you are vegetarian, vegan, or neither, this charming café is a great place for soups, sandwiches, pasta, salads, and some irresistible desserts – all house-made, right down to the delicious multigrain bread.

2 OWL'S NEST BAKERY AND BISTRO
9752 Willow Street, Chemainus; tel: 250-324-8286; www.facebook.com/owlsnestbakerybistro; daily B and L; $
All-day breakfasts (including eggs Benedict, tortillas with slow-braised brisket, poached eggs and trimmings, and yogurt parfait) and lunches (including paninis and crab and shrimp cakes) are served in this charming, friendly spot near the antiques mall.

3 GABRIEL'S GOURMET CAFÉ
39A Commercial Street, Nanaimo; www.gabrielscafe.ca; daily B and L; $$
Supporting local farmers, from whom they buy direct, this café works wonders with all those fresh vegetables and ethically raised meats. There's plenty of choice, including vegetarian options, and lots of international flair.

4 JAVAWOCKY COFFEE HOUSE
90 Front Street, Nanaimo; tel: 250-753-1688; www.facebook.com/javawocky. Coffeehouse daily B and L; $
Right on the waterfront, with seating inside or out beside the Harbourfront Walkway, this place serves great coffee and snacks, including sandwiches and freshly baked treats, including Nanaimo bars.

The boardwalk in the Pacific Rim National Park

PACIFIC RIM NATIONAL PARK RESERVE

Here is an excellent view of the Pacific Coast in all its glory: mountains, coastal rainforest, wild beaches and rocky islands stretching intermittently for 125km (77.6 miles) between the towns of Tofino in the north and Port Renfrew to the south.

DISTANCE: 166km (103 miles), 358km (222 miles) if you include Bamfield

TIME: 3 days (more to explore the Broken Group Islands or walk the West Coast Trail)

START: Port Alberni

END: Ucluelet/Bamfield

POINTS TO NOTE: It's possible to arrive at the park by plane, bus, or even by boat (the *Frances Barkley*). However, most visitors drive. By car, you'll enter the park on Highway-4 from Port Alberni. At "The Junction", where Highway 4 forks south for Ucluelet and north for Tofino, you'll find the Pacific Rim National Park visitor centre. Pay here, or at trailhead parking lots, for national park entry fee (you're in black bear country; pick up a Parks Canada leaflet for information). In Tofino, there are two main concentrations of accommodations: in town or a couple of kilometres south, lining the beaches. Otherwise, try one of the near-town campgrounds. Reservations are a must in summer, when most places have a two- or three-night minimum.

The Pacific Rim National Park Reserve divides into three distinct areas: the most popular Long Beach; the Broken Group Islands, hundreds of islets only accessible to sailors and kayakers; and the West Coast Trail, a tough but popular long-distance hike. The area is also a magnet for surfing and whale-watching.

PORT ALBERNI

Self-proclaimed "Gateway to the Pacific", **Port Alberni ❶** is a lumber town and busy fishing port. Various logging and pulp-mill tours are available, but the town's main interest to travellers is as a base for the Pacific Rim National Park. The route below takes the road; the stretch of Highway 4 from Port Alberni to the park's visitor centre (105km/65 miles) is beautiful, but requires careful driving — much of it is winding and adjoined by sheer drops.

TOFINO

Tofino ❷, once a fishing village, has been dramatically changed by tourism, but retains its natural charm. It erupts

Whale watching off Tofino

into a frenzy during summer and is graced with magnificent views. There are top accommodations and an unexpectedly rich restaurant scene – downtown has a lively café culture and Industrial Way is the place for start-ups.

Drop in at the Roy Henry Vickers Gallery, 350 Campbell St (www.royhenryvickers.com), a gallery housed in a traditional longhouse-style building. Roy sometimes does storytelling here and the place gets packed out – see the homepage of the website for dates. A block away is cash-only **Common Loaf Bake Shop**, see ❶, the perfect low key spot for lunch.

Stay a couple of nights in Tofino (see page 108) and eat dinner Downtown somewhere lively like **Wolf in the Fog**, see ❷. On your second day, take a boat or seaplane tour to the hot springs, or choose whale-watching, surfing (Canada's best surf is close at hand; contact www.surfsister.com) or kayaking (www.paddlewest kayaking.com).

LONG BEACH

On your third day, take a picnic to explore **Long Beach ❸**, a tract of wild sand stretching 30km (18.6 miles) south from Tofino to Ucluelet. The Coastal Mountain Range provides a scenic back-

Whale-watching

The Pacific Rim National Park Reserve is one of the world's best areas for whale-watching, thanks to its location on the main migration routes, food-rich waters and numerous sheltered bays. The season runs from March to late October and it's easy to find a boat going out from Tofino, Ucluelet or Bamfield, most charging around $110 a head for the trip depending on duration (usually 2–3hr). Note that Zodiacs (inflatables), are bouncier, more thrilling and potentially wetter, and rigid-hull cruisers (covered or uncovered), are more sedate. Even if you don't take a boat trip, you stand a slim chance of seeing whales from the coast.

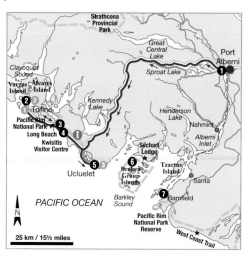

A view over Tofino

Long Beach

drop, while behind the beach lies a lush canopy of coastal rainforest.

Long Beach is noted for its wildlife. As well as the smaller stuff in tidal pools, there are large mammals like whales and sea lions, in addition to thousands of migrating birds. Resist picking up shells as it's against park regulations.

The best way to get a taste of the area is to walk the beaches or forested shorelines; you could follow any of nine well-maintained hiking trails, most of which are short. All the paths are clearly marked from Highway 4, but it's worth picking up a guide from the **Kwisitis Visitor Centre** ❹, located at the southeast end of Wickaninnish Beach.

UCLUELET

Ucluelet ❺ (pronounced you-clue-let) means "safe harbour", from the Indigenous word *ucluth* – "wind blowing in from the bay". It was named by the Nuu-chah-nulth, who lived here for centuries before the arrival of Europeans. Today the port is the third largest in BC by volume of fish landed; but it's not an industrial hub. Instead it has become a destination in its own right, offering similar kayaking, whale- and bear watching opportunities as Tofino but with a laidback, small-town vibe.

Stay overnight (see page 108) and eat hearty fare at **Frankie's Resto-Bar** see ❸; use the next morning to walk the 9km (5.5-mile) Wild Pacific Trail (www.wildpacifictrail.com), which takes you through the rainforest by the ocean. Much of the

The West Coast Trail

The West Coast Trail (WCT) traverses exceptional coastal scenery for 75km (46.6 miles) to Port Renfrew. It requires expertise in backcountry camping, proper equipment and relative fitness. Reckon on six to eight days for the full trip; carry all your food and be prepared for rain, dangerous stretches, and utter isolation.

Mariners long ago dubbed this area the "graveyard of the Pacific". When the SS Valencia went down in 1906 a trail was constructed to guide stranded sailors to safety. The path was open until the 1960s when it fell into disrepair; backpackers reblazed the trail, which now passes through the territory of the Huu-ay-aht First Nation around Bamfield and Ditidaht First Nation country, ending in Pacheedaht First Nation traditional territory near Port Renfrew.

Pre-planning is essential as Parks Canada has a quota system to protect the environment. Numbers are limited to around 7,000 a year while the path is open (May–Sept). July and August are the driest months. Locals will ferry you across some of the wider rivers. You can reserve from January and you'll need to move fast; to make bookings call tel: 250-726-4453, (daily 8am–4pm) or head online to www.pc.gc.ca/pacificrim. Be ready to state the location from which you wish to start, the date of departure, two alternative start dates, credit card details and the number of your party (10 max).

A Giant Pacific Octopus at Ucluelet Aquarium

trail is accessible to wheelchairs and strollers, and there are interactive children's sections along the way. Kids will also love Ucluelet Aquarium (www.uclueletaquarium.org) on the waterfront promenade.

THE BROKEN GROUP ISLANDS

The only way for the ordinary traveller to approach the hundred or so **Broken Group Islands** ⑥ is by seaplane, chartered boat or boat tours; the *Francis Barkley* (June to mid-Sep; tel: 250-723-8313; www.ladyrosemarine.com) departs from Ucluelet at 2pm on Mondays, Wednesdays and Fridays (check online for current schedule). Boats dock at Sechart, where you can stay at Sechart Lodge, a former whaling station. It's not possible to do a day-trip, unless you depart from Port Alberni.

Immensely wild and beautiful, the islands have the reputation for tremendous wildlife, the best kayaking in North America, and some of the continent's finest diving; contact the Pacific Rim National Park information centre (tel: 250-726-4212, www.pc.gc.ca). You can rent kayaks and gear at Sechart – contact Lady Rose Marine Services to check current arrangements. You need to know what you're doing – there's plenty of dangerous water – and you should pick up the relevant marine chart (Canadian Hydrographic Service Chart: Broken Group 3670) onboard the Frances Barkley, or it's available locally (try Pioneer

Boat Works in Ucluelet, 166 Fraser Lane; tel: 250-726-4382).

Food and drink

① COMMON LOAF BAKE SHOP

180 1st Street, Tofino; tel: 250-725-3915; daily B & L; $.

Come sunup, about everyone in town clusters around the heaving tables of the Common Loaf, a solid choice for breakfast, coffee and snacks; after lunch, the house-made dough is turned into pizzas instead of bread and rolls. Cash only.

② WOLF IN THE FOG

150 Fourth Street, Tofino; tel: 250-725-9653, www.wolfinthefog.com; daily D; Sat & Sun B & L; $$$.

Award-winning, two-storey Wolf serves up a seasonal menu of freshly-foraged and locally caught and grown delights such as zingingly fresh poached cod. Downstairs is a lively bar with a superb range of cocktails (try the cedar sour) and local beers.

③ FRANKIE'S RESTO-BAR

1576 Imperial Lane; Ucluelet; tel: 250-726-2225; www.frankiesrestobar.com; Daily D; $$.

Excellent shack offering take-out and eat-in hearty BBQ (served with mashed potato, seasonal veg and cornbread), burgers and pasta. The owner is from Québec so the brisket poutine starter is a no-brainer. Plenty of BC beers and wine on the menu, too.

Comox

NORTHERN VANCOUVER ISLAND

Many visitors head up the east coast of Vancouver Island to travel the Inside Passage or Discovery Passage, two most memorable journeys. Make time for the wild interior, much of it contained within Strathcona Provincial Park.

DISTANCE: 342km (212 miles), or 434km (270 miles) including a side-trip to Strathcona Provinvial Park
TIME: 2–3 days
START: Qualicum Beach
END: Port Hardy (or continue by ferry to Prince Rupert/Bella Coola)
POINTS TO NOTE: Pacific Coastal Airlines (www.pacificcoastal.com) and Central Mountain Air (www.flycma.com) both fly to Campbell River from Vancouver, or you can fly to Port Hardy from Vancouver with Pacific Coastal Airlines (www.pacific-coastal.com), and follow this route in reverse. If you stay close to Port McNeill or Telegraph Cove, you can spend time in Alert Bay, on Cormorant Island. If you're arriving in Port Hardy in summer, there's pressure on hotel accommodation, so it's vital to call ahead if you're not camping or haven't worked your arrival to coincide with one of the ferry sailings.

Along Highway 19 lies the hamlet of Buckley Bay, which consists of little more than a ferry terminal to **Denman and Hornby** islands ❶ (10 round trips daily, 10 min), two outposts that have been described as the "undiscovered Gulf Islands". There's no public transport on either island so you'll need a car or bike; you can expect to encounter eagles, herons, spring wildflowers and lots of aquatic wildlife.

COMOX VALLEY

On Highway 19 north of Buckley Bay is a short stretch of wild, pebbly beach, then the **Comox Valley** ❷. Of three settlements here – Comox, Cumberland and Courtenay – the last is of the most interest.

The Comox Valley scores higher inland, on the eastern edge of Strathcona Provincial Park (see page 90) and the skiing area of Mount Washington (www.mount washington.ca). There's plenty of hiking and mountain biking in summer, especially on Forbidden Plateau. For details, ask at the visitor centre in Cumberland.

CAMPBELL RIVER

Of the myriad Canadian towns that claim to be "Salmon Capital of the World",

Strathcona Provincial Park

Campbell River ❸ is probably the one that comes closest to justifying the boast; you'll need a saltwater fishing licence that you can buy online in advance (www.fishing.gov.bc.ca). The town is home to pre-eminent sushi spot, **Wasabiya Japanese Sushi Café**, see ❶.

QUADRA ISLAND

Quadra Island ❹ and its fine beaches and museum are fifteen minutes from Campbell River; don't miss the Nuyumbalees Cultural Centre (May–Sept daily 10am–4pm; tel: 250-285-3733, www.museumatcapemudge.com) in Cape Mudge Village near the island's southern tip (take Green Road), home to a sacred potlatch collection. While on the island you can laze on its beaches, walk its trails, or climb Chinese Mountain for some cracking views.

STRATHCONA PROVINCIAL PARK

The approach to **Strathcona Provincial Park ❺** along Highway 28 is worth it for the scenery. Elk Falls Provincial Park is the first stop, ten minutes out of Campbell River.

Strathcona Provincial Park is Vancouver Island's largest protected area. The island's highest point, Golden Hinde (2220m/7,283ft) is here, and there's a good chance of seeing rare wildlife such as the Roosevelt elk and black-tailed deer. Only two areas have visitor facilities – Forbidden Plateau and the Buttle Lake region, accessible via Highway 28.

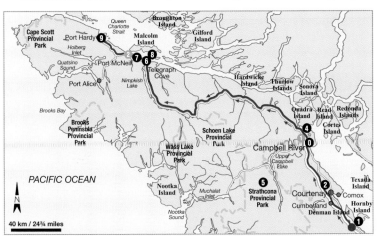

Telegraph cove

CAMPBELL RIVER TO PORT MCNEILL

Return to Campbell River to get back on the main highway. Tiny **Telegraph Cove** ❻ is one of BC's "boardwalk villages", the whole community raised on wooden stilts over the water. It's also a reliable spot to see whales (mid-June to Oct). Contact Stubbs Island Charters (www. stubbs-sightings.com).

Port McNeill ❼, 195km (121 miles) north of Campbell River offers much in the way of whale-watching (Mackay Whale Watching is an excellent local outfit; www.whaletime.com) and Indigenous cultural tours (contact www.seawolfadventures.ca). Stay overnight – the excellent **Cluxewe Waterfront Bistro**, see ❷, is in a resort of the same name – and start out early the next day for Alert Bay.

ALERT BAY

There are frequent ferries from Port McNeill to **Alert Bay** ❽, on Cormorant Island. In migrating season (May–Sept), the crossing offers a chance of spotting whales. Half the island population is Namgis First Nation and a day-visit offers the opportunity to get a glimpse into the history. To the right of the terminal are the totems of a Namgis Burial Ground; you're asked to view from a respectful distance.

Bear left from the terminal to reach the U'Mista Cultural Centre (mid-May to early Sept daily 9am–5pm; rest of the year Tue–Sat 9am–5pm; tel: 250-974-5403,

www.umista.ca) at 1 Front Street, which houses a collection of masks and other sacred items which were confiscated by the government in 1921 and, after years of fighting, have mostly been repatriated.

PORT HARDY

Your final stop, **Port Hardy** ❾ is the

Snow to Surf race

The Comox Valley is about the scenery and outdoor activities, and the Snow to Surf race held in late April has a bit of everything. Teams of nine people compete: A downhill skier runs in ski boots up a slope at Mount Washington, races down the run to hand a baton to a cross-country skier, who speeds through an 8km (5-mile) course to hand off to a runner, who starts running down the mountain, handing off after 7 or 8km (5 miles) to a second runner who heads off on a logging road for about the same distance, leading to the start of the mountain bike leg. Tired yet? The mountain biker heads up into forest for a 12km (7.5-mile) ride. A kayaker awaits at Comox Lake, paddling about 5km (3 mile) to the starting point of the road cyclists, who have a short 30km (19-mile) ride down to the water, where two canoeists wait their turn. The last leg, a 5km (3-mile) paddle in Comox Bay ends at the Comox marina, where team members have congregated to cheer the canoes at the finish line.

Spotting bears on a boat tour from Port Hardy

departure point for ships plying the spectacular stretches of the Inside Passage. If you have time to kill, visit the Quatse Salmon Stewardship Centre (www.the-salmoncentre.org) at 8400 Byng Road.

Adventurous types should join Coastal Rainforest Safaris on a boat tour to spot sea otters, whales and grizzly bears (http://coastalrainforestsafaris.com) or drop in at the visitor centre at 7250 Market Street (www.visitporthardy.com), which has details on Cape Scott Provincial Park (www.env.gov.bc.ca/bcparks).

The ferry terminal (www.bcferries.com) is visible from town but is actually 10km (6.2 miles) away at Bear Cove. Both the Inside Passage to Prince Rupert (15hr) and the Discovery Passage to Bella Coola (summer only, 13hr) are a great way to see grand coastal scenery. Ferries sail every two days; you must book accommodation at your destination before leaving.

Hiking

Hiking is superb in Strathcona, with a jaw-dropping scenic combination of jagged mountains, lakes, rivers, waterfalls and forest. There are several shorter, marked trails accessible from the highway. All the longer trails can be done in a day, though the most popular, the Elk River Trail (10km/6.2 miles) lends itself to an overnight stop; popular with backpackers because of its gentle grade, the path ends up at Landslide Lake, an idyllic camping spot. The other highly regarded trail is the Flower Ridge walk, a steep 14km (8.6-mile) round-trip that starts at the southern end of Buttle Lake and involves a very stiff 1250m elevation gain. In the Forbidden Plateau area, the most popular trek is the Forbidden Plateau Skyride to the summit of Wood Mountain where there's a 2km (1.2-mile) trail to a viewpoint over Boston Canyon.

Food and drink

① WASABIYA JAPANESE SUSHI CAFE
465 Merecroft Road, Campbell River; tel: 250-287-7711; www.wasabiyasushicafe.com; Tue–Fri L & early D, Sat D; $$
Exceptional sushi spot with tempting menu divergences such as chilled noodles with fish cake, seared tuna, and mixed tempura in a hot soup. A thirty-minute drive south of the ferry terminal. Reservations highly recommended; take-out available.

② CLUXEWE WATERFRONT BISTRO
1 Cluxewe Campground Road, Port McNeill; tel: 250-230-1006; www.cluxeweresort.com/bistro; $$$
Incredible spot 9km north of Port McNeill with huge windows framing ocean views over Broughton Strait. Seasonal, local produce and, unsurprisingly given the location, lots of seafood (the scallops are excellent). Although the resort is reopening in 2021, the bistro will remain closed until spring 2022; call ahead for opening times and to make a reservation.

Old Growth Forest around Prince George

HWY-16: PRINCE GEORGE TO PRINCE RUPERT

Highway 16 (part of the epic Yellowhead Highway) travels east–west across Northern BC. The road connects some wonderful communities and includes the glorious river and mountain landscapes of the Skeena Valley.

DISTANCE: 718km (446 miles)
TIME: 2 days
START: Prince George
END: Prince Rupert
POINTS TO NOTE: Air Canada Jazz, CMA and WestJet fly to Prince George from Vancouver. It's also possible to get to/from Vancouver by train with an overnight stay in Jasper (www.viarail.ca), but it takes over two days. The station is downtown at 1300 1st Avenue. Prince Rupert airport (tel: 250-624-6274) is on Digby Island with ferry connections to the BC and Alaska Marine ferry terminals and shuttle bus connections to downtown (tel: 250-622-2222), which leave and drop off at the Prince Rupert Hotel at 118 6 Street. Air Canada Jazz operates a daily service between Prince Rupert and Vancouver (2hr). Inland Air (tel: 250-624-2577, www.inlandair.bc.ca) runs a daily 50min flight to Masset in summer. The ferry terminal for BC Ferries (www.bcferries.com) to Port Hardy and Haida Gwaii is at Fairview Dock at the end of Highway 16. Reservations are essential if you're taking a car.

Most people make this trip as a link in a much longer journey, possibly connecting to ferries to Haida Gwaii (see page 98) or to Port Hardy on Northern Vancouver Island (see page 91). The best place to pause during the journey is near Hazelton, where you can visit a cluster of First Nations villages.

PRINCE GEORGE

Rough-edged **Prince George ❶** is the general area's services and transport centre. Forestry is at the core of its industrial landscape – if you ever wanted the inside story on the lumber business, this is where to find it. Today the city offers a handful of attractions, many of which involve the surrounding forests. The Adventure Bus Tour Company can take you out into the back country for the day, or for overnight back packing and camping, contact Meg (www.theadventurebustours.com).

There are a host of hiking trails that can be tackled independently, not least in the **Ancient Forest/Chun T'oh Whudujut Provincial Park ❷**,

Old red barn near Smithers

the world's furthest inland rainforest. Much closer are 15km (9.3 miles) of trails and a gorgeous lakeside picnic site at Forests for the World.

The luscious greenery and brightly-coloured flowerbeds make central Connaught Hill Park well worth a visit; the park also affords a 360-degree view over the city. Check with the tourist office for directions.

Two fantastic places to visit include the Railway & Forestry Museum at 850 River Road (www.pgrfm.bc.ca) houses the largest vintage rail collection in BC, and Hodul'eh-a: A Place of Learning is dedicated to the Lheidli T'enneh band who have lived on this land for more than 9000 years.

SMITHERS AND AROUND

Drive on toward **Smithers** ❸, the largest community after Prince George, and a picturesque outdoor-adventure hub. The sizeable Swiss population has made its mark on the alpine-themed downtown; **Two Sisters Cafe**, see ❶, is not to be missed.

There is mountain biking and hiking in the Babine Mountains Provincial Park and downhill and cross-country skiing on Hudson Bay Mountain (www.hudson baymountain.ca). For indoor attractions, try the Bulkley Valley Museum (www.bv museum.org) at the corner of Main Street and Highway 16, which has a permanent display on the history of flight in the area.

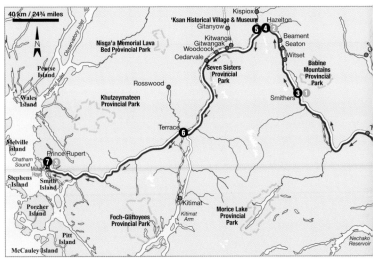

Detail of a longhouse at 'Ksan Historical Village

SKEENA VALLEY

Just beyond Smithers, the Skeena River carves a beautiful valley through the Coast Mountains. For a couple of hours the road and railway run past an imposing backdrop of snow-capped peaks half-reflected in the estuary. Shortly after Highway 16 meets the river near New Hazelton and **Hazelton ❹**, a couple of minor roads strike off to four nearby villages, where something of the culture of the Indigenous Gitxsan peoples has been preserved. Close to Hazelton, there's decent accommodation to break your journey (see page 109), and delicious roadside coffee and cake is available at **Zelda's Travel Mug Café**, see ❷, in New Hazelton.

FIRST NATIONS VILLAGES

A few kilometres off Highway 16, on the High Level Road out of New Hazelton, the **'Ksan Historical Village & Museum ❺** is the site of an entire reconstructed Gitxsan village (tours daily Apr–Sept 9am–5pm; tel: 250-842-5544; www.ksan.org). Guides take visitors around seven cedar longhouses and numerous totem poles, providing commentary, insight and history on the carvings, buildings and masks on show.

Kispiox, 13km (8 miles) north of Hazelton, is the ancient Gitxsan home of the Frog, Wolf and Fireweed clans. Locals prefer the traditional village name, Anspayaxw, meaning "people of the hidden

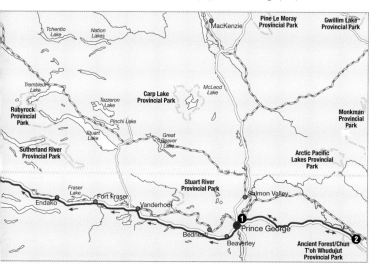

place". The highlights are 15 riverside totems, some of which can be spotted in Emily Carr's iconic paintings. For more totems, Gitanyow's 18 poles include the 140-year-old "Hole in the Sky". You can sometimes watch poles being repaired at the village's two carving sheds.

TERRACE

Some 144km (90 miles) beyond Hazelton, Highway 16 passes through **Ter-race** , the commercial centre of the Skeena Valley. On the road here, you'll spot the spectacular peaks of Seven Sisters Provincial Park; some trail-heads are signposted from Highway 16, including the easy 3km (1.8-mile) Watson Lakes trail. You can ski at Shames Mountain (mid-Dec to mid-April; tel: 250-635-3773; www.mymountaincoop.ca) or take a trip to a genuine ghost town (www.northernbcjetboattours.ca).

PRINCE RUPERT

There's a bracing tang of salt and fish in the air in **Prince Rupert** that will really wake you up and blow away the cobwebs! Prince Ruperts itself is a distinctive port on Kaien Island. A stunning place when the mist lifts, it looks out over an archipelago of islands and is ringed by mountains that tumble to the sea along a beautiful fjord-cut coastline. In the summer, cruise ships make pit stops here, spewing up to two thousand passengers ashore to gorge on fish and chips. There's plenty of outdoor and indoor attractions, and it's an amiable spot to while away a day. Some of the highlights include tours of the world-renowned Khutzeymateen Grizzly Bear Sanctuary (see page 97) and a stop at the Museum of Northern British Columbia.

MUSEUM OF NORTHERN BRITISH COLUMBIA

Prince Rupert's excellent Museum of

The aurora borealis

The aurora borealis, or Northern Lights, is a beautiful and ethereal display in the upper atmosphere that can be seen over large areas of northern Canada. The aurora was long thought to be produced by sunlight reflected from polar snow and ice, and certain Inuit believed the lights were the spirits of animals or ancestors; others thought they represented wicked forces. Research still continues into the phenomenon, and while the earth's geomagnetic field certainly plays some part in the creation of the aurora, its source would appear to lie with the sun.

You should be able to see the Northern Lights as far south as Prince George. They are at their most dazzling from December to March, though they are potentially visible year-round. Look out for a faint glow on the northeastern horizon after dusk, and then – if you're lucky – for the full show as the night deepens.

Northern British Columbia (June–Sept daily 9am–5pm; Oct–May Tues–Sat 9am–5pm; tel: 250-624-3207, www.museumofnorthernbc.com) is housed in an impressive reproduction Indigenous cedar longhouse on 1st Avenue at McBride Street. The museum is particularly strong on the culture and history of the local Tsimshian and is ideal ways to whittle away a wet afternoon. A short walk from the museum is **Cowpuccino's Coffee House**, see ❸.

MOUNT HAYS

Hike up here for a bird's-eye view of the harbour and the chance to spot bald eagles. To reach the steep track providing the only route to the top, take the Wantage Road turn-off on Highway 16 just out of town. It's three hours to the top but you get good views after clambering a short way up the track.

Grizzly Bear Sanctuary

A very popular trip from Prince Rupert is the 6hr boat tour to Khutzeymateen Grizzly Bear Sanctuary (best time mid-May to early Aug), a remote coastal valley created in 1994 to protect BC's largest-known coastal population of grizzly bears – the damage done to grizzly habitats by logging, mining, hunting and other concerns is one of the keenest environmental issues in the province. In the summer, several local tour operators run full-day and multi-day boat tours to view the grizzlies on the water's edge. For a seven-hour trip contact Prince Rupert Adventure Tours (www.adventuretours.net), or if you have three days and plenty of spare change, get in touch with Khutzeymateen Wilderness lodge (www.khutzlodge.com).

Food and drink

❶ TWO SISTERS CAFÉ

3763 Fourth Avenue, Smithers; tel: 250-877-7708; http://twosisterscafe.ca; Mon–Sat B & L; $$.

Breakfast is a highlight, but also try their great artisan breads, smoothies, soups and wraps. They support local farmers and growers, and go the extra step to be sustainable.

❷ ZELDA'S TRAVEL MUG CAFÉ

Hwy-16 New Hazelton; tel: 250-842-5444; www.facebook.com/zeldastravelmugcafe; Tue–Thu & Sun B & L, Fri & Sat B, L & D; $.

Roadside licensed coffee bar with sandwiches, paninis and wraps on the menu, and daily specials like chicken pot pie. Great desserts, too.

❸ COWPUCCINOS

25 Cow Bay Road, Prince Rupert; tel: 250-627-1395; daily B & L; $.

A relaxed café with local character serving fair-trade coffee, fresh soups, sandwiches and home-made desserts. Open mic nights and live music occasionally, too.

Bonanza Beach on Graham Island

HAIDA GWAII

Arranged in a gentle arc off the Prince Rupert coast, Haida Gwaii consists of a triangular-shaped archipelago of two major islands – Graham and Moresby – and two hundred islets that make an enticing diversion from the heavily travelled sea route up through BC's coast.

DISTANCE: 277km (172 miles), plus trip to Gwaii Haanas
TIME: 2 days
START: Queen Charlotte
END: Queen Charlotte
POINTS TO NOTE: The islands can be accessed by air from Vancouver or by ferry or air from Prince Rupert. Flights land at Masset on Graham Island or Sandspit on Moresby Island. Ferries from Prince Rupert dock at Skidegate Landing on Graham Island. Demand for accommodation is high (see page 109). BC Ferries (www.bcferries.com) plies between Graham Island (Skidegate) and Moresby Island (Alliford Bay) with regular crossings (10 daily; 7am–5.30pm; foot passengers and cars). There is no public transport on the island but taxis and shuttles are available. Car hire rates run to about $50 a day plus mileage. Contact Budget Car Rental at Skidegate Airport (tel: 250-637-5688), Island Auto Rentals in Queen Charlotte (tel: 250-559-4118), or Masset Car and Truck Rentals (tel: 250-626-7089).

The islands are something of a cult destination; the Gwaii Haanas National Park Reserve and Haida Heritage Site protects large tracts of land, incredible biodiversity, traditional villages and numerous archeological sites. Most casual visitors stick to Graham Island, where the bulk of the islands' roads are concentrated along its eastern side. Moresby Island is all but free from human contact except for the small logging community of Sandspit.

QUEEN CHARLOTTE

Graham Island's second-largest settlement, **Queen Charlotte ❶**, is a good place to base yourself. The village takes its name from the ship of Captain George Dixon, the British explorer who sailed to Haida Gwaii in 1787.

For a fine overview, try the hike (3–5hr) to the top of Sleeping Beauty Mountain; the trailhead is reached by a rough forest road accessible (ideally by a vehicle with high clearance) from Crown Forest Road near Honna Road. The visitor centre at 3220 Wharf Way (tel: 250-559-

8316; www.queencharlottevisitorcentre.com) is the place to organize fishing, sailing, sightseeing and canoeing trips. Just across the road you can get decent pub grub at **Ocean View Pub & Grill**, see ❶.

HAIDA HERITAGE CENTRE AT KAAY LLNAGAAY, SKIDEGATE

Drive east on Ocean View Drive and beyond Skidegate Landing is the **Haida Heritage Centre at Kaay Llnagaay** ❼ (Mon–Sat, plus Sun in summer; tel: 250-559-7885; www.haidaheritage centre.com). You can browse aspects of Haida culture at the centre – a series of longhouses fronted by totem poles, including an art and carving studio and a museum which contains a collection of the Haida's treasured argillite carvings.

> ## "Canadian Galapagos"
>
> Some areas of Haida Gwaii were one of only two tracts in western Canada to escape the last Ice Age, which elsewhere altered evolutionary progress; this enabled the survival of many so-called endemics, species which aren't found anywhere else in the world. Those unique to the islands include a fine yellow daisy, the world's largest subspecies of black bear, and the hairy woodpecker. There's also a good chance of spotting several species of whale, otter, sea lion and other aquatic mammals, schools of fish and a host of colourful marine invertebrates.

TLELL

Take a deserted dune stroll on East Beach in **Tlell** ❸, home to the only glamping site

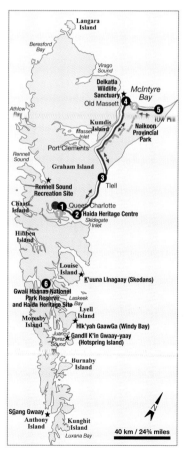

Exploring one of the forests of Haida Gwaii

on the islands (see page 109).

Tlell is at the southern border of the Naikoon Provincial Park, an enclave designed to protect the fine beach, dune and dwarf-woodland habitats. You can walk numerous trails along the beach and through the forests.

OLD MASSETT

The village of **Old Massett** ❹ is where some 800 Haida live and work. For more information on where to see carving,

---

The Haida

The Haida were feared warriors, paddling into rival villages and returning with canoes laden with goods and slaves, and Haida villages were an impressive sight, their vast cedar-plank houses dominated by 15-metre totem poles. Equal elaboration attended the many Haida ceremonies, one of the most important being the memorial potlatch, which served to mark the end of mourning for a dead chief.

After European contact the Haida population was devastated by smallpox and other epidemics. In 1787, there were approximately 10,000 Haida; by 1915, the population totalled just 588. They were forced to leave many of their traditional villages, where artefacts were appropriated by collectors. Today the 3,000 Haida who live mostly in Old Massett and Skidegate play a powerful role in the islands' social, political and cultural life.

---

visit the Old Massett Council office at 348 Eagle Avenue (Mon–Fri 9am–5pm; tel: 250-626-3337), where you should also enquire about permission to visit the Duu Guusd Heritage Site and Conservancy, established to protect villages on the coast to the northwest, two of which are active. The park is a base for the Haida Gwaii Rediscovery Centre.

Drive back through Masset and stop downtown at the food truck, **Moon Over Naikoon**, see ❷, en route to Tow Hill.

TOW HILL

Walk the trails around **Tow Hill** ❺, 26km (16 miles) east of Old Massett. Three trails begin by the Hiellen River; easiest is the 1km (0.6-mile) Blow Hole Trail, which drops down to striking rock formations and basalt cliffs by the sea. From here you can follow a path to the top of Tow Hill for views of deserted beaches stretching into the distance – on a clear day you can see Alaska. The third track, the Cape Fife Trail, is a longer (10km or 6.2 miles one-way) hike to the east side of the island.

GWAII HAANAS NATIONAL PARK RESERVE AND HAIDA HERITAGE SITE

Return to Queen Charlotte and stay overnight. Next day, visit **Gwaii Haanas National Park Reserve and Haida Heritage Site** ❻; access is only by boat or chartered seaplane. If you have just one day, Haida Style Expeditions (tel:

Waves crashing on Graham Island

250-637-1151; www.haidastyle.com) take visitors from Queen Charlotte on an open-air zodiac (they provide wet weather gear), or Inland Air Charters (tel: 250-624-2577, www.inlandair.bc.ca) offer full-day flight and boat tours. For longer boat or kayak tours, contact the Queen Charlotte Visitor Centre. You must make a reservation and attend an orientation session. Contact Parks Canada for updated times and locations (www.pc.gc.ca/gwaiihaanas).

Food and drink

① OCEAN VIEW PUB & GRILL

3200 Oceanview Road; Queen Charlotte; tel: 250-559-8503; Wed–Fri D; Sat & Sun L & D; $$

As lively a place as you'll find round here, the bar and grill has a respectable selection of brews and great menu with a seafood focus, including fish and chips. There are regular band performances and karaoke nights.

② MOON OVER NAIKOON

Tow Hill Road, 9km (5.6 miles) east of Masset; tel: 250-626-9344; B & L; $

Inexpensive pizza slices, soup, and their famous "cinny" cinnamon buns, served on an old school bus in the sticks. There's a simple shelter outdoors (with hammocks) or you can eat in the cosily converted interior. Look out for the red barn and then take the second right. Cash only. Mid-May to Sept only.

Haida Heritage Site

Gwaii Haanas National Park Reserve and Haida Heritage Site, located on the southern portion of Haida Gwaii, is a 90km (56-mile) -long archipelago of 207 islands, some 600 Haida archeological sites, five Haida Gwaii Watchmen village sites and 1,750km (1,087 miles) of coastline.

Visits to a variety of ancient Haida village sites and their totems are described here in order of distance from Sandspit. Closest is K'uuna Llnagaay (Skedans), accessible by boat from Moresby Camp; access to the camp is by logging road. Farther afield are T'aanuu Llnagaay, Hlk'yah GaawGa (Windy Bay) and Gandll K'in Gwaay-yaay (Hotspring Island), whose series of outdoor thermal pools make it one of the most popular destinations. The finest site is the furthest away: SGang Gwaay (Ninstints) is close to the southern tip of the archipelago. Residents left around 1880 in the wake of smallpox epidemics and today it contains the most striking of the ruined Haida villages; the moss-covered depressions where longhouses once stood, and the many mouldering mortuary totems are a UNESCO World Heritage Site. In accordance with the wishes of the Haida, little attempt is made to preserve ancient village sites and, within decades, many of these decaying totem poles may have returned to nature.

DIRECTORY

Hand-picked hotels and restaurants to suit all budgets and tastes, organised by area, plus select nightlife listings and an overview of the best books and films to give you a flavour of the city.

ACCOMMODATION

There's a huge range of accommodation in Vancouver and the rest of BC, including some of Canada's finest luxury hotels, major international chains, motels, bed-and-breakfasts, and vacation rentals. In remote areas, accommodation tends to be basic (wi-fi is often an additional charge), and can be scarce in summer. Local tourist offices have useful lists of accommodation, sometimes available online. For hotels close to Vancouver or Victoria waterfronts, nightly rates can be in excess of $500 in high season. If you're on a low budget, you're better off in the hostels, the excellent YWCA, or a less-central location as inexpensive hotels can be dingy and in sketchy areas. Remember when budgeting to factor in parking; you'll pay a daily fee, usually in the $30–50 range, even in the hotels' own parking lots or garages.

The majority of in-city campsites are for RVs only, but there are opportunities to camp on some of the out-of-city routes. 175 of BC's provincial parks have campgrounds; for further information, call 1-800-689-9025, or make reservations online at https://discover camping.ca..

Vancouver: Waterfront and Downtown

Auberge Vancouver Hotel

837 West Hastings Street; tel: 604-678-8899/1-855-678-8998; www.aubergevancouver.com; $$$.
Well placed for waterfront attractions, this luxurious boutique hotel offers great views, a spa and pool, and a daily supply of chocolates.

Fairmont Hotel Vancouver

900 West Georgia Street; tel: 604-684-3131; www.fairmont.com; $$$$
In 2019 this already splendid 'Castle in the City' unveiled the result of a $55 million restoration project. The Heritage Suites on the 14th floor are particularly palatial.

Vancouver: Chinatown and Gastown

Skwachàys Lodge

31 West Pender Street; tel: 604-687-3589; www.skwachays.com; $$$
You'll spot the soaring totem pole on the rooftop before you arrive at Vancouver's only First Nations-run hotel and gallery, which offers a chance to learn more about Indigenous arts and culture amid plenty of mod cons.

Price for a standard double room for one night in high season
$ = under $150
$$ = $151–300
$$$ = $301–500
$$$$ = over $500

Decor at Skwachàys Lodge

Victorian Hotel

514 Homer Street; tel: 604-681-6369; www.victorianhotel.ca; $$$

This is a charming old building with 21st-century comforts and contemporary boutique style inside. Some rooms feature old brick walls and is a 5-minute walk from the Gastown Steam Clock.

Vancouver: Yaletown and Granville Island

Granville Island Hotel

1253 Johnston Street; tel: 605-683-7373/800-663-1840; www.granvilleislandhotel.com; $$$

This is the only hotel on the Granville Island, and it's a beauty – right on the waterfront, and with various sizes of attractive and comfortable rooms and suites, some with balconies.

YWCA Hotel Vancouver

733 Beatty Street; tel: 604-895-5830/800-663-1424; www.ywcavan.org/hotel; $$

Across from BC Place, this bright, modern hotel has a social purpose: profits help women with families out of poverty. It has a wide range of room sizes, not all with private bathrooms.

Vancouver: Stanley Park

Listel Hotel

1300 Robson Street; tel: 04 684 8461; www.thelistelhotel.com; $$$$

A boutique art hotel, the Listel has an eco-friendly edge and lashings of originality. Its museum floor, a collaboration with the Museum of Anthropology, has original Indigenous art and rooms on the Gallery floor are mini art galleries featuring international and Canadian artists. The Artist Series suites represent different artists and design movements.

Sylvia Hotel

1154 Gilford Street; tel: 604 681 9321; https://sylviahotel.com; $$

An ivy-wrapped landmark in a heritage building, this popular place has an excellent reputation and unbeatable location, at the beach two blocks from Stanley Park.

Squamish

Howe Sound Inn & Brewing Company

37801 Cleveland Avenue; tel: 604-892-2603; www.howesound.com; $$$

This cozy place is in the town centre, but still has great views from some of the rooms, and there's a craft brewery, restaurant, and sauna on site. Continental breakfast is included.

Squamish Adventure Inn

38220 Highway 99; tel: 604-892-9240; www.squamishhostel.com; $

This is a great-value and wonderfully friendly hostel in a good location for exploring nearby trails and adventure activities, including their own slack-lining setup. It has dorms and private rooms, a shared kitchen, and well-kept public areas.

Clean lines at the Listel Hotel

Whistler

Crystal Lodge & Suites Hotel
4154 Village Green; tel: 844-343-9023; www.crystal-lodge.com; $$$
Close to the gondolas, this hotel has a great central location, a wide variety of room types, a pool, sauna and hot tub, underground parking, and a cluster of restaurants and stores..

Pangea Pod Hotel
4333 Sunrise Alley; tel: 844-726-4329; www.pangeapod.com; $$
A cross between a designer boutique and a hostel, this unusual and unique place has sociable public areas and pods where you sleep, consisting of basic curtain-shielded compartments with a mattress on the floor. You need to be agile to occupy an upper pod.

Summit Lodge Boutique Hotel
4359 Main Street; tel: 604-932-2778/888-913-8811; www.summitlodge.com; $$$$
In a good central location, the sleek modern studios and suites here have subdued décor with pops of colour. Food options include tapas and sushi and various pamperings are offered in the spa.

The Okanagan

Barefoot Beach Resort
4145 Skaha Lake Road, Penticton tel: 778-476-0484, www.barefootresort.ca; $
Set directly on the shores of Skaha Lake with spacious pristine camp sites, RV hook-ups, and beautifully equipped yurts on-site. The resort boasts a licensed restaurant, market, ice cream and taco shop, beachwear store, plus a beachfront coffee and juice bar and Canada's only on-beach Crossfit gym

Hiawatha RV Park
3795 Lakeshore Road, Kelowna tel: 250-861-4837/888-784-7275, www.hiawatharvpark.com; $
Reasonably close to the action and backing onto Lakeshore Road, with a separate tent area, laundry, heated pool and free hot showers. March–Oct only.

Prestige Hotel
1675 Abbott Street, Kelowna tel: 250-860-7900, 877-737-8443; www.prestigehotelsandresorts.com; $$
Across from City Park and close to the beach, this is one of the best options in town. Rooms have modern, country-style furnishings, and there's access to an indoor pool, hot-tub and fitness centre, plus a bar, and a seafood restaurant.

Revelstoke, Golden and Field

Williamson Lake Campground
1818 Williamson Lake Road, 3km (2 miles) south of Revelstoke; tel: 250-837-5512; www.williamsonlakecampground.com; $
Pleasant, fifty-site lakeside campground south of the town centre, near the airport. There are free hot showers, flush toilets, laundry, a beach, canoe and rowing boat rentals and a mini-golf course. Sites $30, RVs $35

Pangea Pod Hotel

Cathedral Mountain Lodge

Yoho Valley Road, 5km (3 miles) northeast of Field; tel: 250-343-6442/866-619-6442; www.cathedralmountain.com; $$$$

This fabulous collection of luxury log cabins is beautifully situated in the lee of Cathedral Mountain, 3km (2 miles) off Highway 1. Ideally placed for exploring the Yoho Valley, with no phones or TVs to distract you from the incredible scenery. Late May to early Oct only.

Truffle Pigs

100 Center Street, Field; tel: 250-343-6303; www.trufflepigs.com; $$

Elegant hotel whose rooms have a contemporary boutique feel and sweeping views of the Kicking Horse Valley. Some have kitchens and sleep up to six, but one big bonus is that only lodge guests can reserve a table at Truffle Pigs Bistro (see page 115).

(see page 115)

Victoria

Magnolia Hotel & Spa

623 Courtney Street; tel: 250-381-0999/877-624-6654; www.magnoliahotel.com; $$$

This 64-room boutique hotel lays on the period Edwardian character thick, but it's never stuffy about it. High-quality rooms, the best of which boast harbour views and fireplaces, have superb bathrooms, and the on-site spa is one of the best in the city.

Fairmont Empress

721 Government Street; tel: 250-384-8111; www.fairmont.com; $$$$

One of the finest hotels in the world, the Fairmont embodies colonial grandeur, even down to its famous afternoon teas. A $60 million restoration in 2017 ensured up-to-the-minute features.

Inn at Laurel Point

680 Montréal Street; tel: 250-386-8721/800-663-7667; www.laurelpoint.com; $$$

Don't be deterred by the size of this resort-style hotel. All the rooms have a balcony and a good harbour view, and the contemporary aesthetic is a far cry from the chintzy look of many of Victoria's hotels. Opt for a room in the southern wing, designed by Arthur Erickson.

Duncan

Thunderbird Motel

5849 York Road; tel: 250-748-8192/877-748-8192; www.thunderbirdmotorinn.ca; $

Near the theatre, recreation centre, and aquatic centre, and just two blocks from downtown, this is a friendly (and pet-friendly) motel with spacious air-conditioned rooms. Some rooms have a kitchenette.

Valley View Bed and Breakfast

2277 Quamichan Park Road; tel: 250-748-5484/250-701-3557; $$

There's a really lovely view over the Cowichan Valley countryside from this pleasant little B&B with high ceilings, large windows, and a picturesque garden. It has just three letting bedrooms and children are welcome.

Room at the Fairmont Empress

Nanaimo

Buccaneer Inn

1577 Stewart Avenue; tel: 250-753-1246/
877-282-6337; thebuccaneerinn.com; $
A family-run motel close to the ferry terminal. Studios, suites and kitchenette
rooms are spotless, and perks include a
barbecue, laundry, and storage for bikes.

Coast Bastion Hotel

11 Bastion Street; tel: 250-753-6601/800-
716-6199; $$
Perfectly situated between the inner
harbour and Commercial Street, this
hotel has rooms with water views. The
seafood restaurant, Minnoz, does a
mean salmon eggs Benedict.

Tofino

Ecolodge at Tofino Botanical Garden

1084 Pacific Rim Highway tel: 250-725-
1220; www.tofinobotanicalgardens.com; $$
Eight of the 11 rooms at this eco-minded
facility have shared baths, resulting in
a pleasing price tag (at least by Tofino
standards). There's also a bunk room
for four who don't mind sharing. The setting – at the heart of the town's botanical
garden – is picturesque, the communal
kitchen large and inviting, and the library
(there are no TVs) well-stocked.

Chesterman Beach B&B

1345 Chesterman Beach Road; tel: 250-
725-3726; www.chestermanbeach.net; $$$
Three luxurious oceanfront suites on the
beach with private entrance, kitchen-
ettes and bathrooms, one of which, the
Garden Cottage, has a truly lovely pri-
vate garden. Off season rates plummet.

Ucluelet

Black Rock Oceanfront Resort

596 Marine Drive tel: 250-726-4800/877-
762-5011; www.blackrockresort.com; $$$
Luxurious, all-suite hotel where floor-to-
ceiling windows and balconies overlook
lanky pine trees and crashing surf. All
studios and suites include a kitchenette.

Wya Point

2695 Tofino Ucluelet Highway, 5km (3
miles) from Ucluelet; tel: 250-726-2625;
www.wyapoint.com; $
Idyllic, peaceful Indigenous-owned and
run eco-retreat set on 600 acres (243
hectares) of old-growth forest on a private beachfront. Options range from
cosy yurts and well-equipped lodges
with barbecue, fireplace and spectacular views to RV hook-ups and camping.

Northern Vancouver Island

Hidden Cove Lodge

Lewis Point, a secluded cove on Johnstone
Strait 14km (8.5 miles) from Telegraph Cove;
tel: 250-956-3916; www.hiddencovelodge.
com; $$
A stay here feels like you've moved to a
nature reserve: sea lions, otters, grizzly
bears and porpoises are all frequently
spotted on the secluded property. The
main building has nine units, and three
cabins facing the Johnstone Strait.
Breakfast and dinner is served in the cav-
ernous dining room. Open May–Oct.

Suite at the Magnolia Hotel & Spa

Ecoscape Cabins

6305 Jensen Cove Road, Port Hardy; tel: 250-949-8524; www.ecoscapecabins.com; $$
Beautifully constructed, environmentally-friendly cabins built from salvaged cedar. All come with kitchenettes, flat-screen TVs, and access to barbecue grills and fire pits; the fanciest one has a washer-dryer and sleeping loft. Polished stones line the shower floors and there's a bubbling stream fronting the cabins.

Prince George to Prince Rupert

Coast Inn of the North

770 Brunswick Street, Prince George; tel: 250-563-0121/800-716-6199; www.coasthotels.com; $
One of the more luxurious hotels in town, with 155 rooms. Guests have access to a spa, hair salon, and a choice of fine dining at its three restaurants.

Bulkley Valley Motel

4444 Hwy-16, New Hazelton; tel: 250-842-6817/888 988 1144; www.bvmotel.ca; $
Clean, cosy and quiet with air-conditioned rooms, each of which is equipped with a kitchen, TV and internet access. Laundry facilities and four restaurants are within easy walking distance.

Trakehner Hof B&B

236 Glen Meadow Road, 15km (9 miles) north of Hazelton; tel: 250-842-8077; www.trakehnerhof.ca; $$
Located close to the Skeena River, this three-room B&B offers modern and comfortable quarters with breathtaking views of the surrounding valley and mountains. Horseriding, totem-pole tours and fishing excursions are also on offer.

Haida Gwaii

Premier Creek Lodging

3101 3rd Avenue; Queen Charlotte; tel: 250-559-8415/888-322-3388; www.premiercreek.ca; $$
The first-choice hotel in town is a restored 1910 heritage building overlooking the harbour and Bearskin Bay. Some single rooms are available, with a shared bathroom.

Sword Fern Inn

3127 2nd Avenue, Queen Charlotte; tel: 250-626-9299; www.swordferninn.com; $$
An intimate inn that has a deck offering expansive views of the harbour from its hill vantage point. There's a fire pit and barbecue in the garden which adds to a homely and friendly atmosphere, and the place strives to be eco-friendly.

Haida Gwaii Glamping Co

Hwy-16, Tlell; tel: 778-674-7711; www.haidagqaiiglampingco.com; $$$
These luxurious timber framed tents are a cut above the rest. Each "tent" has a double bed with soft bamboo bedding, en-suite baths and views of the forest or ocean. A continental breakfast is provided, and there are barbecues, a crab-cooking pot, and a geodesic dome "social house" with an oven, fridge, dishwasher, sinks and ice machine.

Dishes at ARC

RESTAURANTS

If you want to eat well, you'll be spoilt for choice in British Columbia – and you won't have to spend a fortune. This West Coast province enjoys the flavours of Asian cuisines (superlative sushi in particular), as well as the British-imported penchant for joints of meat and hearty stews. Seafood is particularly good, including wild salmon, oysters, and sweet local spot prawns. Vancouver's restaurants are some of the country's finest: they led the trend in nose-to-tail, seed-to-stem dining and you'll find plenty of fresh local produce. BC wines consistently win major international awards and many of the province's wineries have restaurants serving food of a similarly outstanding standard.

Vegetarians, vegans, and the gluten-intolerant are well served in the big cities, not only by a number of specialist places but also an increasing number of mainstream restaurants that are adding suitable items to their menus, though in more remote areas choice is limited. Many sustainable programs, including Green Table, whose member restaurants commit to reduced waste and more recycling, more eco-friendly practices, and more products that benefit the local economy, were pioneered here before being launched in the rest of the country.

Food truck mania

The food truck scene in Vancouver and on Vancouver Island is particularly vibrant. Trucks offer a culturally diverse range of cuisines, healthy options, and comfort food. In Vancouver, Mom's Grilled Cheese is usually at the top of any list of favorites, and is usually parked at Howe and Robson streets. Other popular trucks include Tacofino, Vij's Railway Express, Japadog, Roaming Dragon, and Aussie Pie Guy. In Victoria, Deadbeetz tops the list, and Taco Justice, L'Authentique Poutine Burgers, Finest at Sea, and Greek on the Street, are among the most popular. The whereabouts the trucks on any specific day can be found at https://street-foodapp.com (as well as Vancouver and Victoria, they cover Whistler, Squamish, Comox Valley, Nanaimo, Kelowna and Prince Rupert). Click on any coloured dot on the map there and it will give you the name of the truck and its location.

Price for a two-course meal for one including a glass of wine (or other beverage)
$ = under $20
$$ = $20–45
$$$ = $45–60
$$$$ = over $60

Vancouver: Waterfront and Downtown

ARC Restaurant
Fairmont Waterfront Hotel, 900 Canada

Place; tel: 604-691-1818; www.arcdining.com; daily B, L and D; $$$$

Locavore devotees will be delighted to hear about the produce from the hotel's rooftop garden and the honey from its own beehives. It doesn't get much more local than that in the heart of a city. Seafood from nearby waters figures large on the menu.

Cactus Club Café

1085 Canada Place; tel: 605-620-7410; www.cactusclubcafe.com; daily L and D; $$$

This branch of the West Coast chain, noted for its casual fine dining, has a prime location within Canada Place, looking out over the floatplane dock and the mountains of North Vancouver. It has a refined and varied menu ranging from filet mignon to sandwiches to sablefish to vegan-friendly plant-based dishes.

Miku

70–200 Granville Street, Corner of Canada Place and Howe Street; tel: 604-568-3900; https://mikurestaurant.com; daily L and D; $$$

Modern Japanese food here includes a huge range of creative Aburi sushi, nigiri, and sashimi. All kinds of accolades have been heaped on this place over the years, and they are well-deserved. Take-out and deliveries are available too.

Hawksworth Restaurant

Rosewood Hotel Georgia, 801 West Georgia Street; tel: 604-605-8282; http://hawksworthrestaurant.com; daily B, L and D; $$$

Set in Vancouver's most distinguished hotel, chef David Hawksworth, several times Vancouver Magazine Chef of the Year, serves exquisite Canadian cuisine amid voguish chandeliers with an impressive wine cellar and one of the city's finest cocktail bars. Signature dishes include crispy skin wild salmon with pistachio crumble and white asparagus

Hy's Steakhouse

637 Hornby Street; tel: 604-683-7671; https://hyssteakhouse.com; Mon–Fri L and D, Sat & Sun D; $$$$

Hang the expense and dig into mouth-watering Alberta steaks, dry-aged for a month, paired with ambrosial sides like creamed spinach, their legendary cheese toast for two, or a classic Caesar salad made table-side.

Vancouver: Chinatown and Gastown

Bao Bei Chinese Brasserie

163 Keefer Street, at Main, Chinatown; tel: 604-688-0876; www.bao-bei.ca; Wed–Sun D; $$

Wildly popular upscale Chinese fusion restaurant. It's a gorgeous space: dim lighting, plenty of vintage design details like old lamps and armoires with friendly servers and delicious craft cocktails. Standout items include handmade dumplings and beef tartare.

Classy Giardino Restaurant

Chambar

568 Beatty Street, Gastown: tel: 604-879-7119; www.chambar.com; Wed–Fri D, Sat & Sun B, L and D; $$$

On the edge of Chinatown, off West Pender Street, this is a reliable choice serving luscious heaped servings of moules-frites, delicately spiced tajines and from 8am to 3pm, superb Belgian waffles with toppings like bacon-caramel and white chocolate pistachio rosewater.

The Flying Pig

102 Water Street, Gastown; tel: 604-559-7968; https://theflyingpigvan.com; daily L and D; $$

A popular place right on the main tourist route through Gastown, offering succulent steaks and interesting seafood dishes, like the blackened steelhead trout with ragu of prawns, chorizo, and pasta or crab-crusted white sturgeon with squash and barley risotto. Other outlets in Yaletown and Olympic Village.

Meat & Bread

370 Cambie Street, Gastown; tel: 604-566-9003, www.meatandbread.com; Mon–Sat L; $

Hip, habit-forming sandwich shop famed for its porchetta sandwich – thick slices of slow-roasted, crispy pork doused with salsa verde, crammed into fresh bread, and served with fancy mustard. The tiny menu also includes a vegetarian sandwich. Three other outlets in Vancouver.

Phnom-Penh

244 East Georgia Street, near Gore; tel: 604-682-5777; daily L and D; $$

Excellent, cheap Vietnamese and Cambodian cuisine – legendary for their deep-fried chicken wings, in a friendly, family-oriented restaurant.

Wildebeest

120 West Hastings Street, Gastown; tel: 604 687 6880; https://wildebeest.ca; $$

This is possibly the quintessential Gastown restaurant, offering nose-to-tail dining, excellent brunch, and decidedly moreish craft cocktails. Although this is an unashamedly meat-centric restaurant, vegetarians are well taken care of.

Vancouver: Yaletown & Granville Island

Brix & Mortar

1138 Homer Street; tel: 604-915-9463; www.brixandmortar.ca; Wed–Sun D; $$$

In a historic brick building (with another entrance at 1137 Hamilton Street), this two-story restaurant has a patio downstairs and a glass-covered courtyard on the upper level. The menu is modern Canadian, with interesting flavors cooked into the wild salmon, free-range chicken, AAA steaks, and other top quality farm-fresh meats.

Giardino Restaurant

1328 Hornby Street; tel: 604-669-2422; http://umberto.com/giardino; Tue–Sat D; $$$$

Upscale, loud, and very expensive, this

restaurant has a long and interesting menu, with mains like slow oven-braised veal ossobuco with saffron rice and grilled Ahi tuna with pickled ginger and orange glaze.

The Greek by Anatoli

1043 Mainland Street; tel: 604-979-0700; https://thegreekbyanatoli.com; Mon–Fri L and D, Sat & Sun late L and D; $$
One of three in Vancouver (the others in Gastown and North Vancouver), this is a lively and fun Greek meze restaurant with one of Yaletown's best-located patios. Service is engaging and the menu features popular favorites – keftedes, moussaka, souvlaki – and lesser known options that are well worth trying.

Minami Restaurant

1118 Mainland Street; tel: 604-685-8080; https://minamirestaurant.com; daily L and D; $$$$
The sister restaurant of Miku (see page 111), this place melds Japanese and West Coast cuisine, with innovative sushi and subtle flavoring of the meat dishes. If the cuisine is new to you, the two chef's tasting menus provide a perfect introduction.

Dockside Restaurant

1253 Johnston Street, Granville Island; tel: 604-685-7070; https://docksidevancouver.com; daily B, L and D; $$$
Floor-to-ceiling windows make the most of the fabulous view from this contemporary restaurant, as does its waterfront patio. Their menu has plenty of choice, including salads, seafood, and meats and beverages include beers from their own brewery.

Vancouver: Stanley Park

For restaurants within the park, see page 46. The following are in the West End neighborhood next to the park.

Buckstop

833 Denman Street; tel: 604-428-2528; http://buckstop.ca; Mon–Fri D; Sat & Sun L and D; $$
Decadent barbecue and small plates tavern offering up the West End's finest late-night eats and craft cocktails made with local spirits, fruits, and herbs. The menu has plenty of pocket-pleasing options: the fried dill pickles are fantastic and the barbecue assortment for $15 offers three different meats.

Forage

1300 Robson Street; tel: 604-661-1400; https://foragevancouver.com; daily B and D; $$
This is a casual farm to table bistro with an outstanding eco-ethic and warm, friendly service. The menu regularly changes to reflect the best seasonal, local ingredients, but their award-winning sustainable seafood chowder is always on the menu and a must-have. The brunch here is a West End institution.

Potato and bacon wood-fired pizza at a Whistler restaurant.

Kingyo

871 Denman Street; tel: 604-608-1677; www.kingyo-izakaya.ca; daily L and D; $$

The city's most elaborate lunch bento box is to be found here, but they only make 10 and they sell out every day, so arrive early. In the boisterous restaurant, the welcome is warm and loud, with Asian-influenced cocktails and dishes such as tuna *tataki*, stone-grilled beef tongue, and crunchy *ebi* (prawn) mayo.

Whistler

Araxi

4222 Village Square; tel: 604-932-4540; www.araxi.com; Daily D; $$$

A top-rated restaurant of long standing that serves Italian and West Coast-style food, with inventive pasta, a high-quality raw bar and seafood dishes with out-standing service. The wine list runs to 27 pages and 9000 bottles, and there's a good choice of wines by the glass. For a more budget experience, come for the daily oyster specials 3–5pm.

Braidwood Tavern

4591 Blackcomb Way; tel: 604-966-5280; www.braidwoodtavern.com; Daily B, L, and D; $$$

Casual dining and après ski at communal tables in this new restaurant-bar inspired by a traditional mountainside tavern. Mains include burgers, steelhead trout and pizza with interesting sounding toppings like elk salami and aragula.

Purebread

Olympic Plaza; tel: 604-962-1182; www.purebread.ca; Daily B and L; $

Outstanding bakery with innovative sweet and savoury treats, serving up Portland's Stumptown Coffee. The line can be long but it's absolutely worth it; you'll likely happen upon raspberry scones, salt caramel bars, caramel-frosted cinnamon buns and "pudgie pies" (roasted potato and goat's cheese tucked inside a plump pocket of puff pastry).

The Okanagan

Roberto's Gelato

Suite 227, 15 Park Place, Osoyoos; tel: 250-495-5425; www.robertosgelato.com; Daily L; $

The searingly hot temperatures Osoyoos often experiences make this top-notch ice-cream bar an essential stop-off. Home-made using all natural ingredients. May–Oct only.

Brodo Kitchen

483 Main Street, Penticton tel: 250-476-1275; www.tastebrodo.com; Mon–Sat L and early D; $

Simple food made with locally sourced ingredients, changed seasonally. Basic soups, salads and sandwiches are the order of the day, but oh, so very well done. The albacore tuna melt is a thing of beauty and the soups are addictive; ordering a flight of three is highly recommended.

The Broken Anchor

2355 Gordon Drive, Kelowna; tel: 250-763-3474; www.brokenanchorseafood.ca; Daily L and early D; $$

Sustainable seafood spot with a patio where you can eat heaped-high portions of zingingly fresh seafood at decent prices, and beach-ready picnic packs to takeout. Local beers, ciders and wine by the bottle.

Revelstoke, Golden and Field

Village Idiot

306 MacKenzie Avenue, Revelstoke; tel: 250-837-6240; www.thevillageidiot.ca; Wed–Mon L & D; $$

Locals' favourite hangout year-round, which attracts a big ski-season crowd too. The suntrap patio gets packed, so come early to bag a table. Excellent pizzas, sandwiches, burgers and customizable piled-high poutines.

Eleven 22

1122 10th Avenue S, Golden tel: 250-344-2443; www.eleven22restaurant.com; Daily D; $$

Hip and popular restaurant with an oft-changing but always eclectic menu (pastas to curries to fondues), but whose great strength is Asian food. The Dragon Boat – scallops, prawns and mussels in a smoky paprika red wine sauce – is delicious. With a lovely outdoor patio.

Truffle Pigs Bistro

100 Center Street, Field; tel: 250-343-6303, www.trufflepigs.com; daily B, L & D; $$

The coffee shop here opens at 9am, followed by the full bistro for lunch and dinner. It's an unpretentious family-run affair with dishes made from local produce and décor featuring flying pigs. Snacks, home-baked breads and cakes, but the dinner menu is the highlight: beef bourguignon along with the offbeat likes of black truffle pierogies.

Victoria

The Fish Store

Fisherman's Wharf, 1 Dallas Road; tel: 250-383-6462; https://floatingfishstore.com; daily L and early D, closed in winter; $$

The fish is not only 100 percent Ocean Wise, it could not be fresher, coming from their own attached licensed processing plant on the Inner Harbour. This also cuts out the middle-man and ensures great pricing. A superb salmon chowder, gently steamed shellfish, traditional fish and chips, fish tacos, rice wraps, and sandwiches are all on offer.

Hank's *A Restaurant

Unit G2A 1001 Douglas Street; tel: 778-433-4770; www.hanksarestaurant.com; Tue–Sat 5–10pm; $$

Pull up a stool at the counter in this tiny blink-and-you'll-miss-it joint. Ethically produced meat only on the menu – including their own pigs and turkeys from the Comox Valley – but also they might also serve mussels in a nduja and wine sauce or pork hock with leek, apple and cabbage.

Generous portions at Jam Café

Jam Café

542 Herald Street; tel: 778-440-4489; http://jamcafes.com; daily B and L; $$

The line out the door is a reflection of the quality and choice within, so arrive early and be prepared to wait. Once inside, there's an enormous menu, including more than 30 breakfast choices, and soup, mac-and-cheese, and generously filled sandwiches for lunch.

Duncan

Alderlea Farm and Café

3390 Glenora Road; tel: 250-597-3438; www.alderleafarm.com; mid-Mar–late Oct, Fri–Sun L and D; $$

It's a little way outside of Duncan, but it's worth making the trip to eat here to enjoy their farm-fresh food. In addition to great wood-fired pizzas, dishes include roast chicken and beef and veggie burgers. If you have children, they'll enjoy meeting the animals.

Craig Street Brew Pub

25 Craig Street; tel: 250-737-2337; www.csbrewery.ca/craigstreetbrewpub; Mon–Thu 11am–11pm, Fri–Sat until midnight, Sun until 10pm; $$

Beer brewed on site accompanies well-executed pub-food classics, and there's a very welcoming atmosphere. It's a good place to mingle with the locals too.

Chemainus

Thai Pinto Cuisine

9875 Maple Street; tel: 250-324-8424; daily L and D; $$

If you like Thai food, you won't be disappointed here. Authentic dishes are nicely presented in generous portions and it's a very friendly place too. The pad Thai, red curry, and green papaya salad come highly recommended.

Nanaimo

Longwood Brewpub

5775 Turner Road, 11km (6.5 miles) north of Downtown (off Island Hwy); tel: 250-729-8225; www.longwoodbrewpub.com; daily L and D; $$$

Atmospheric brewpub with fireplaces, pool tables, darts, and views of the Vancouver Island mountains from the outdoor deck. The beer, lovingly brewed on-site, is excellent, and the sophisticated pub fare is nothing to sniff at either.

Penny's Palapa

10 Wharf Street; tel: 250-753-2150; www.pennyspalapa.com; daily L and D; $$

A great place to replenish your energy after a harbourfront walk, this floating Mexican restaurant is filled with open-air umbrella-topped tables, colourful flower pots, and warm blankets for when the sea breeze blows. The menu emphasizes organic produce, and the margaritas are made from scratch. It's very popular and petite, so arrive early for dinner.

Pirate Chips

#1, 75 Front Street; tel: 250-753-2447; http://piratechips.ca; Thu–Mon D; $$

Here's the place to try the deep-fried Nanaimo bar – in fact, almost everything

is deep fried at this heart-stopping hangout with kooky maritime décor. Expect chilli fries, *poutine*, and fish and chips on the menu. Portions are generous, and gluten-free, vegan, and vegetarian options are available.

Tofino

RedCan Gourmet

700 Industrial Way; tel: 250-725-2525; www.redcangourmet.com; Wed–Sun L and early D; $$

Set in an industrial part of town, the outwardly humble RedCan fires up extraordinary takes on Pacific Rim cuisine such as cumin-scented seafood chowder and their popular "Dirty" mac'n'cheese with bbq beef brisket, as well as Tofino's best pizza. There are a handful of chairs, but most patrons head here for takeout. Limited hours in the off-season.

Shelter

601 Campbell Street; tel: 250-725-3353; www.shelterrestaurant.com; Daily L and D; $$$

A favourite for locals and visitors alike, this lodge-like hot-spot is where foodies, locavores, city slickers and surfers all rub elbows over "surf bowls" (wild salmon, teriyaki sauce and basmati rice), warm chèvre salad with braised greens and mussels pulled up by town fishermen.

Ucluelet

Ukee Dogs

1576 Imperial Lane; tel: 250-726-2103; Daily L; $

Friendly and cheap hot-dog hut with innovative combinations such as a mac and cheese dog, and the "whole hog", slathered with pulled pork, onions, barbecue sauce and cheddar. Beer on tap, too.

Prince George and Prince Rupert

Ramen Ya Sendo

Bon Voyage Plaza, 4488 Hwy-16, Prince George; tel: 250-964-6771; Tue–Sun L and early D; $

Previously Sendo Sushi, this much loved local spot serves up slurpable ramen (gluten free and vegan also available) and freshly made gyoza.

White Goose Bistro

1205 3rd Avenue, Prince Rupert; tel: 250-561-1002; www.whitegoosebistro.ca; Mon–Sat L and D; Sun D; $$$

For high-quality food, try this white tablecloth bistro, specializing in Italian and French cuisine – try the lobster ravioli, ribeye steak, or duo of duck. They also have an express lunch menu with great fish tacos.

Waterfront Restaurant

222 1st Avenue West at Crest Hotel, Prince Rupert; tel: 250-627-6771; www.cresthotel.bc.ca; Daily B, L, and D; $$$

Enjoy the region's finest northwest-coast cuisine with a tantalizing menu featuring local seafood, steaks and pasta while enjoying the view of the bald eagles soaring outside.

NIGHTLIFE

Vancouver is a big, vibrant city with nightlife to match, whether it's serious theatre, comedy, dance clubs, or live music bars and pubs. The action is spread around several neighbourhoods: Granville Street is a downtown hub, lit up by neon, with bars and clubs open until the early hours and a young crowd out on the street in between venues. Yaletown and Gastown are more sophisticated, where people gather for cocktails or a relaxed meal. Main Street and Commercial Drive have a couple of dance clubs and a thriving craft beer and restaurant scene, while Davie Village is a particularly LGBTQ-friendly area, although just about every venue is welcoming to all.

Victoria has an equally diverse range of cocktail bars, brewpubs, live music venues and clubs, although not quite so many, and Douglas Street is a good place to start. Elsewhere in BC, Whistler enjoys year-round nightlife and après-ski activity, and places like Kelowna, Nanaimo and Prince Rupert have a smattering of nightlife and performance arts options – although you're unlikely to be travelling to the interior or north of the province for night-time fun, most BC towns have at least a bar. In remote areas, evening entertainment revolves around drinking in the local hotel bar.

Theatres and Concert Halls

Vancouver
Arts Club Theatre
Main box office at 1585 Johnston Street; tel: 604-687-1644; www.artsclub.com.
A leading light in the city's drama scene, performing at three venues: the Stanley Industrial Alliance Stage, 2750 Granville Street, is the company's main venue and runs larger musicals, modern classics and acclaimed productions from around the world; the Granville Island stage offers mainstream drama, comedies and musicals; the next-door Revue Stage shows small-scale revues and cabaret.

Orpheum
601 Smithe Street; tel: 604-665-3035; https://vancouvercivictheatres.com
A grand, ornate theatre with 2,672 seats, this is the city's principal concert hall hosting international performers as well as the Vancouver Symphony.

Playhouse
600 Hamilton Street; tel: 604-665-3038; https://vancouvercivictheatres.com
With 668 seats, this theatre is a more intimate space in which to enjoy chamber music, dance, film, and plays.

Queen Elizabeth Theatre
630 Hamilton Street; tel: 604-665-2193; https://vancouvercivictheatres.com

Water Street in Vancouver's Gastown on a busy Friday night

Hosting Broadway musicals, opera, ballet, and more, this is one of the city's foremost theatres.

Victoria
The Belfry Theatre
11291 Gladstone Avenue; tel: 250-385-6815; www.belfry.bc.ca
Around a dozen plays are staged here every year.

Langham Court Theatre
805 Langham Court; tel: 250-384-2142; www.langhamtheatre.ca
Out in the Rockland neighbourhood, this theatre has been running for around 90 years, staging popular plays and comedies.

Royal Theatre
805 Broughton Street; tel: 250-361-0800; www.rmts.bc.ca
This 1913 theatre is the city's largest performance arts space; sister to the McPherson Playhouse at 3 Centennial Square.

Bars and Pubs

Vancouver
The Alibi Room
157 Alexander Street, corner of Main; tel: 604-623-3383; www.alibi.ca
On the edge of Gastown, this place has a craft beer focus, with guest beers from all over BC and elsewhere. They also have local boutique and organic wines and cocktails, all in a historic building.

BC Kitchen
Parq Vancouver, 39 Smithe Street, tel: 778-370-8300; www.parqvancouver.com/restaurants/bc-kitchen
This is a sophisticated place with a lounge ambience, in spite of the TVs. It provides classic comfort food, craft beers, and cocktails.

Cinema Pub
901 Granville Street; http://donnellygroup.ca/cinema
This stylish place on Theatre Row has a jukebox, a pinball machine, shuffleboard, and sports on TV. It's open until 3am every night.

Fountainhead Pub
1025 Davie Street, West End; tel: 604-687-2222; http://thefountainhead-pub.com
A popular and pleasantly buzzing gay bar at the heart of Davie Village with good food, drink and a large, heated patio. Tends to attract a slightly older, more mellow crowd.

Keefer Bar
135 Keefer Street, Chinatown; tel: 604-688-1961; www.thekeeferbar.com
A lively "apothecary" cocktail bar serving "prescriptions" made from house-made bitters, teas, syrups and infusions with herbs drawn from Traditional Chinese Medicine.

Victoria
Bard & Banker
1022 Government Street; tel: 250-953-

9993; https://bardandbanker.com
Live music every night, with an acoustic 'unplugged' series on Sunday nights.

The Canoe BrewPub

450 Swift Street; tel: 250-361-1940; www.canoebrewpub.com
One of the city's most popular places to eat and drink, with an impressive setting – this was once Victoria's power station, and the interior retains an old industrial feel, with sturdy walls and vast beams. The patio is superb, with views toward the harbour.

Clive's Classic Lounge

740 Burdett Avenue; tel: 250-361-5684; https://clivesclassiclounge.com
Sublime cocktail bar shaking up some of Canada's best mixed drinks. The bitters are house-made, the juice freshly squeezed, and the lengthy drink list adventurous.

The Irish Times

1200 Government Street; tel: 250-373-7775
There's live music every night here, played by local regulars and visiting acts in a mix of genres – Celtic, blues, classic rock and other kinds.

Spinnakers Gastro Brewpub

308 Catherine Street; tel: 250-386-2739
The city's first-ever brewpub is a lively and friendly place in a waterfront heritage building. In addition to great craft beers, there's farm-to-table food and regular events include weekly Celtic music jams, quiz nights, and launch parties every time there's a new brew on tap.

Comedy Clubs

Vancouver
Vancouver TheatreSports League

1515 Anderson Street; tel: 604-738-7013; www.vtsl.com
This place has professional improv comedy in an intimate space on Granville Island.

Yuk Yuk's

2837 Cambie Street; tel: 604-696-9857; www.yukyuks.com
Some of the best-known names in comedy started out at Yuk Yuk's, and standards remain high, even on amateur nights.

Victoria
Hecklers Bar & Grill

123 Gorge Road East; tel: 250-381-1312; www.hecklers.ca
Weekend comedy nights at this spot north of downtown. Dark exterior, friendly staff and inexpensive pub food.

Nightclubs

Vancouver
Celebrities Night Club

1022 Davie Street; tel: 604-681-6180; http://celebritiesnightclub.com
Established in the 1980s, this split level LGBTQ-friendly club has high ceilings,

Venue on Granville Street in Vancouver

state-of-art sound system and visuals, DJs, and live performances.

Fortune Sound Club
147 East Pender Street, Chinatown; tel: 604-569-1758; www.fortunesoundclub.com
All types of Vancouverites mingle at this Chinatown dance club spinning old-school hip-hop, soul, house and others till the small hours.

The Roxy Cabaret
932 Granville Street; tel: 604-331-7999; www.roxyvan.com
A Vancouver institution with DJs, live bands, and lines to get in.

Venue
881 Granville Street; tel: 604-646-0064; http://venuelive.ca
A two-floor club with a great sound systems and light show.

Victoria
Distrikt
919 Douglas Street; tel: 250-220-8587; www.distriktclub.ca
Bumping, laser-lit dance club which is part of the Strathcona Hotel. Varied live bands, including the occasional big name, and nightly dancing.

Upstairs Cabaret
15 Bastion Square; tel: 250-385-LIVE
Top touring DJs spin Top-40 remixes and brilliant live bands provide the music in this fun-loving, friendly venue. Special events are also sometimes hosted here.

Live Music

Vancouver
Commodore Ballroom
868 Granville Street; tel: 604-739-4550; www.commodoreballroom.com
A famous venue with a reputation for big-name acts from both sides of the Atlantic, this long-established venue continues to thrive.

Guilt & Company
1 Alexander Street, Gastown; www.guiltandcompany.com
This is the venue for a little bit of everything; a wide range of styles hit the stage here, from rock and blues to singer-songwriters to jazz.

Victoria
Hermann's Jazz Club
753 View Street, between Douglas and Blanshard; tel: 250-388-9166; www.hermannsjazz.com
Dimly lit club thick with 1950s atmosphere that specializes in Dixieland but has occasional excursions into fusion and blues.

Lucky Bar
517 Yates Street; tel: 250-382-6826; www.luckybar.ca
For live local music, this is the place to be: all stripes of bands pack in here alongside DJs, hip-hop karaoke and other fun nights. Monday evenings are especially popular, when DJs get the crowd dancing with '90s tunes.

MacLeod's Books in Vancouver

BOOKS AND FILM

Books

There have been no books about or set in British Columbia that have hit the *New York Times* bestseller list. However, it's simply not that there are no authors committing their province to paper, and many are well worth reading. Timothy Taylor's 2001 novel, *Stanley Park*, about a father and son relationship, was winner of the One Book, One Vancouver competition in 2004 – his 2011 novel *Blue Light Project* also includes snapshots from Vancouver. And *Song Over Quiet Lake* by Sarah Felix Burns, is a captivating story of a friendship between a Vancouver woman in her 20s and a charming and irrepressible Tligit elder in her 80s.

Two writers from the Chinatown community have provided a unique perspective in their writings: *The Jade Peony* by Wayson Choy is a historical novel set in 1930s Chinatown, as seen through the eyes of three young children, and *Salt Fish Girl* by Larissa Lai portrays a dystopian future Vancouver from a Chinese immigrant's perspective.

Victoria and Vancouver Island has also influenced its writers. *Innocent Cities* by Jack Hodgins, is set partly in Victoria and partly Australia during the late 19th century, and features an aspiring architect and a larger-than-life hotel owner. Then there are the Silas Seaweed mysteries, written by Stanley Evans. This series of books is set in Victoria and features a savvy First Nations (Coast Salish) police officer called Silas Seaweed, who brings a dash of Indigenous mythology to his policing and an insight into a Victoria that tourists don't see. But if you read just one book about Indigenous culture in British Columbia, make it *They Called Me Number One*, a 2013 memoir by Bev Sellars, former councillor and chief of the Xat'sull (Soda Creek) First Nation in Williams Lake, about her childhood experience in the Indian residential school system.

Finally, we must not overlook Douglas Coupland, the prolific Vancouver author who found international success – and added a new phrase to our vocabulary – with his 1991 bestseller, *Generation X: Tales for an Accelerated Culture* (his novel *City of Glass* includes essays and photographs of his home city), or Vancouver and Victoria's connections to Alice Munro; the first Canadian Nobel Prize in Literature winner lived here for more than twenty years and kept a second home in Comox, Vancouver Island, all of her life.

Films

Location shoots in Vancouver and the rest of BC (particularly the beaches and rainforests of Vancouver Island

An outdoor cinema in Stanley Park during summer

and the wintry landscapes in the far north) have been so numerous over many years that the city shares the nickname 'Hollywood North' with Toronto, and remote communities are used to seeing famous faces pop up. However, while BC has developed a fine reputation for pretending to be somewhere else, there really haven't been any major box-office success stories for movies that are actually set in the province or have told a BC-related story.

The same cannot be said for movie actors, though – several big names you will certainly have heard of hail from Vancouver, including Ryan Reynolds, Michael J Fox, Seth Rogen, Cobie Smulders, and Pamela Anderson.

But of course, in the movie world, being a blockbuster is not necessarily the yardstick by which quality is measured; there have been some smaller titles who have seen success, such as *Eve and the Fire Horse* (2005), which picked up a Sundance Festival award. Written and directed by Julia Kwan, this film is an engaging, sometimes humorous, sometimes emotional story about the nine-year-old daughter of Chinese immigrant parents in Vancouver, and her relationship with her relatives and their customs, quirks, and religions. Recognisable filming locations around Vancouver included Chinatown and Coquitlam, a suburb which lies out to the east of the city.

Julia Kwan went on to make an atmospheric documentary about Vancouver's Chinatown – *Everything Will Be* – in 2014, which explores the ways in which the neighborhood is changing and how its residents are being affected.

Other offerings have included David Ray's sci-fi drama, *Fetching Cody* (2005), set in Vancouver's Eastside and featuring a hapless, homeless protagonist who uses a time-traveling chair to return to a time before his girlfriend's drug overdose and prevent it from happening. A homeless young man also featured in Robert Altman's creepy *That Cold Day in the Park* (1969) – this time, the man is taken in and kept captive by a wealthy woman, played by Sandy Dennis. And more recently, *Haida Gwaii: On the Edge of the World*, is an award-winning 2015 feature documentary film about people trying to live in harmony with these remote islands.

Film buffs who are interested in finding out more will discover an in-depth look at contemporary film in British Columbia by checking out local contributions to the Vancouver Short Film Festival (January; www.vsff.com), Vancouver Island Short Film Festival (February; www.visff.com), Victoria Film Festival (February; www.victoriafilm-festival.com), Vancouver International Film Festival (September–October; viff.org), and Whistler Film Festival (December; www.whistlerfilmfestival.com).

ABOUT THIS BOOK

This *Explore Guide* has been produced by the editors of Insight Guides, whose books have set the standard for visual travel guides since 1970. With top-quality photography and authoritative recommendations, these guidebooks bring you the very best routes and itineraries in the world's most exciting destinations.

BEST ROUTES

The routes in the book provide something to suit all budgets, tastes and trip lengths. As well as covering the destination's many classic attractions, the itineraries track lesser-known sights, and there are also excursions for those who want to extend their visit outside the city and region. The routes embrace a range of interests, so whether you are an art fan, a gourmet, a history buff or have kids to entertain, you will find an option to suit.

We recommend reading the whole of a route before setting out. This should help you to familiarise yourself with it and enable you to plan where to stop for refreshments – options are shown in the 'Food and Drink' box at the end of each tour.

For our pick of the tours by theme, consult Recommended Routes for… (see pages 6–7).

INTRODUCTION

The routes are set in context by this introductory section, giving an overview of the destination to set the scene, plus background information on food and drink, shopping and more, while a succinct history timeline highlights the key events over the centuries.

DIRECTORY

Also supporting the routes is a Directory chapter, with our pick of where to stay while you are there and select restaurant listings; these eateries complement the more low-key cafés and restaurants that feature within the routes and are intended to offer a wider choice for evening dining. Also included here are some nightlife listings and our recommendations for books and films about the destination.

AUTHOR AND PROOFREADER

Rachel Mills is a freelance writer, editor and broadcaster based by the sea in Kent. She is a co-author for Rough Guides to New Zealand, India, Canada, Ireland and Great Britain; a contributor to Telegraph Travel, the Independent, AFAR, DK Eyewitness and loveEXPLORING.com; and an expert in sustainable, responsible tourism. Follow her @rachmillstravel on Twitter and Instagram and listen to her radio show Over Here on http://ramsgateradio.com.

Penny Phenix has worked in travel publishing for many years, both in England and in her current home in New Brunswick, Canada, and has written or contributed to many books about Canada. Penny would like to thank her good friend Nancy Cantaffio for her invaluable help with the Vancouver walks featured in this book.

CONTACT THE EDITORS

We hope you find this Explore Guide useful, interesting and a pleasure to read. If you have any questions or feedback on the text, pictures or maps, please do let us know. If you have noticed any errors or outdated facts, or have suggestions for places to include on the routes, we would be delighted to hear from you. Please drop us an email at hello@insightguides.com. Thanks!

CREDITS

Explore Vancouver and BC

Editor: Annie Warren

Author: Rachel Mills

Proofreader: Penny Phenix

Head of DTP and Pre-Press: Rebeka Davies

Head of Publishing: Sarah Clark

Picture Editors: Tom Smyth & Michelle Bhatia

Cartography: Katie Bennett

Photo credits: Accor 8MC, 16, 102ML, 102MC, 102MR, 102MC, 102/103T, 104, 108, 110; Andrew Strain/Grouse Mountain 8/9T; Atlific Hotels 102MR, 109; Britannia Mine Museum 55L, 54/55; Craig Minielly/Aura Photographics 105; Craig Street Brew Pub 19L; Destination Canada 26MC, 93; Evaan Kheraj 17; Four Seasons Hotels & Resorts 102ML; Getty Images 33; Great Bear Lodge 92; Helene Cyr 116; iStock 4MC, 4MR, 6TL, 6ML, 7T, 7M, 10, 11, 12, 14, 20, 26ML, 26MC, 26ML, 26MR, 40, 41, 42, 44/45, 46, 54, 57, 58, 75, 78, 83; Jiri Siftar 1; Joe Mabel 76; Kevin Arnold 4ML; KK Law 8MR; Luis Valdizon 112; Pangea Pod Hotel 107; Photo by Sean Lee on Unsplash 21; Shutterstock 4ML, 4MR, 4/5T, 6MC, 6BC, 7MR, 7MR, 8ML, 8ML, 8MC, 13, 15, 18, 18/19, 22, 23, 24/25, 26MR, 26/27T, 28/29, 30, 31, 32, 34, 35, 36, 37, 38/39, 43, 44, 45L, 47, 48, 49L, 48/49, 50/51, 52, 53, 56, 59L, 58/59, 60/61, 62, 63L, 62/63, 64, 65, 66, 67, 68/69, 70/71, 72, 73, 74, 77, 79, 80, 81, 82, 84, 85, 87L, 86/87, 88, 89, 90, 91, 94, 95, 96/97, 98, 99, 100, 101, 111, 114, 115, 117, 118, 119, 120, 121, 122, 123; The Listel Hotel 106; Welbert Choi 113; West Coast Aquatic Safaris 4MC, 8MR, 86

Cover credits: Vancouver skyline at sunset *Shutterstock*

Printed in China

DISTRIBUTION

UK, Ireland and Europe
Apa Publications (UK) Ltd
sales@insightguides.com

United States and Canada
Ingram Publisher Services
ips@ingramcontent.com

Australia and New Zealand
Booktopia
retailer@booktopia.com.au

Worldwide
Apa Publications (UK) Ltd
sales@insightguides.com

SPECIAL SALES, CONTENT LICENSING AND COPUBLISHING

Insight Guides can be purchased in bulk quantities at discounted prices. We can create special editions, personalised jackets and corporate imprints tailored to your needs.
sales@Insightguides.com
www.insightguides.biz

INDEX

MAP LEGEND

● Start of tour	🚊 Skytrain station	🕯 Lighthouse
— Tour & route direction	✈ Airport	❋ Viewpoint
❶ Recommended sight	🚌 Main bus station	🚡 Cable car
❷ Recommended restaurant/café	✉ Main post office	⚓ Beach
★ Place of interest	⊕ Hospital	Important building
❶ Tourist information	Ⓜ Museum	Transport hub
--- Ferry	📚 Library	Park
—··— International border	✝ Church	Pedestrian area
	🎭 Theatre	Urban area
	𝟏 Statue	Glacier
	▲ Summit	National Park